GEORGIA HISTORY IN OUTLINE

D1598518

Georgia History in Outline

Revised Edition

Kenneth Coleman

THE UNIVERSITY OF GEORGIA PRESS

ATHENS

Copyright © 1978 by the University of Georgia Press
Athens, Georgia 30602

Library of Congress Cataloging in Publication Data

Coleman, Kenneth.
Georgia history in outline.
Bibliography.   p.
Includes index.
1. Georgia–History.   I. Title.
F286.C75 1978   975.8   78-14047
ISBN 0-8203-0467-0

First edition, 1955
Second edition, 1960
Third edition, 1978

00 99   P 11 10 9

Contents

	Preface	vii
I	Colonial Georgia	1
II	Georgia in the Revolution	15
III	Ante-Bellum Georgia, 1785–1860	29
IV	Slavery, Secession, and the Civil War	48
V	Reconstruction, Bourbonism, and Populism, 1865–1900	69
VI	Twentieth-Century Georgia	94
	Bibliography	119
	Index	125
	Maps	130

Preface

THIS volume was prepared to fill the need for a concise history of Georgia. It assumes a knowledge on the part of the reader of the major movements in United States history and attempts to show their application in Georgia and their revelance to its historical development. In the interest of brevity, many well-known and interesting details of Georgia's past have been omitted. Earlier editions were published in 1955 and 1960. The present edition affords the opportunity to make needed revisions and to bring the history up to the present day.

I wish to thank Carl Mauelshagen, head of the History Department, and Horton Burch, dean of the School of General Studies, of the Atlanta Division, University of Georgia (now Georgia State University) for help and encouragement in preparing the original edition. I also owe a debt of gratitude to my coauthors of *A History of Georgia* (Athens, 1977) and the University of Georgia Press for assistance with the present edition.

KENNETH COLEMAN

History Department
The University of Georgia

GEORGIA HISTORY IN OUTLINE

CHAPTER ONE

Colonial Georgia

W H E N white men came to the southeastern part of North
America in the late sixteenth century, the land had taken on
the physical characteristics that it has kept since except for the
changes that man has made. Georgia is divided into three geographic regions: The southern half of the state is coastal plain,
low and relatively sandy; in earlier geological ages it was un-
derneath the sea. North of the coastal plain is the Piedmont
Plateau, a land of rolling hills, red clays, pine and hardwood,
and much good soil if it is not allowed to wash away into the
sea—Middle Georgia in local nomenclature. In the extreme
north are the Appalachian Mountains, a region of tall peaks,
deep and secluded valleys, and hardwood forests. Throughout
the colonial period only the coastal area and land easily accessible to navigable rivers were settled or exploited by the whites.
The entry into the rich Piedmont, just west of Augusta, did not
begin until 1773, the eve of the Revolution.

SETTLEMENT

Though Hernando de Soto had visited Georgia in his
1539–1542 explorations and other Europeans had sailed
along its coast, its first European settlers were Spanish soldiers
from St. Augustine who established an outpost upon St.
Catherines Island in 1566. Soon soldiers and Jesuit priests
founded presidios and at least two missions on the coastal islands. The Jesuits were replaced by Franciscan friars who la-
bored for God and king in Guale, the Spanish name for coastal
Georgia, for the next century. At missions which dotted the
coast and became centers of Spanish civilization and influence,
the Indians were Christianized and taught to live a settled agricultural life under the watchful eyes of devoted friars backed
by the government and soldiers in St. Augustine.

English claim to Georgia was first made in 1663 when Charles II granted the Carolinas, extending as far south as St. Augustine, to eight Lord Proprietors; but occupation and control remained in Spanish hands until the missions and presidios were abandoned in 1686 because of trouble from Carolinians, Indians, and pirates. Georgia's coast now became a battleground between the English and Spanish, both backed by Indian allies. This conflict was especially intensified during the War of the Spanish Succession, 1701–1713, and did not end until the Spanish evacuation of Florida in 1763.

Everybody has heard the well-worn and persistent story that Georgia was founded for the relief of debtors languishing in English prisons. In reality, no committee ever visited the English prisons to choose settlers for the new colony. If any released debtors were sent to Georgia it was because they happened to be among the hundreds of poor and unemployed making application and were considered by the Trustees to be deserving of aid and promising as colonists. There were three motives behind English colonization of Georgia: humanitarian and philanthropic concern for the unfortunate, debtors and non-debtors, of England and the Protestant areas of Europe; imperial defense and desire to gain control of the unsettled lands between South Carolina and Spanish Florida; and the mercantilistic idea of procuring land where products needed in England but not produced in the British Empire could be acquired. Increase in the English Indian trade and the gaining of the friendship of the Southern Indians in the triangular duel between England, France, and Spain would help equally well imperial advancement and mercantilism.

The eighteenth century was a period of great humanitarian effort to help the unfortunate. One of England's leading humanitarians was Dr. Thomas Bray, a clergyman who had lived in America. A friend of Dr. Bray's, James Edward Oglethorpe, became interested in conditions in English prisons and was made chairman of a Parliamentary committee to investigate prison conditions. A vigorous inspection acquainted the public with the bad conditions of the prisons and secured considerable improvement as well as the release of many unfortunate prisoners.

Released prisoners were often in little better condition, because of the bad environment in which they had to live. Bray had favored founding a colony to help people released from debtors' prisons but died before any action could be taken. In the summer of 1730 a group of prominent men, including friends of the late Dr. Bray and led by Oglethorpe and John Viscount Percival (later Earl of Egmont), petitioned the king for a tract of land "on the south-west of Carolina for settling poor persons of London." A charter, granted on June 9, 1732, created twenty-one "Trustees for establishing the colony of Georgia" who should manage the new colony. Georgia was granted the lands between the Savannah and Altamaha rivers, and lines were drawn from their headwaters to the Pacific Ocean.

The imperial defense phase of the founding of Georgia had two distinct parts. The better known, the struggle between the Spanish and the English to secure control of the "debatable land" between the Carolina settlements and St. Augustine, has already been recounted. The second—and perhaps more important though not so well known—phase concerned the attempt of the English to secure from the Spanish and French the trade of the Southern Indians living between the Atlantic and the Mississippi. Whoever controlled this trade profited economically and generally enjoyed friendly relations with the Indians. Charleston Indian traders were especially desirous of controlling the trade and having the friendship of the Creeks, the largest and most important Southern Indian tribe, who lived in what is today the southern part of Georgia and Alabama. Physical control of the area would help control the Indians and their trade.

Another economic reason for the settling of Georgia was that it would help the British Empire to become more fully mercantilistic. Silk production had been tried with little success in Virginia and the Carolinas and was still considered important enough to be put forward as one of the main reasons urged for the founding of Georgia. Hopes of producing wine, spices, and other semi-tropical plants were also voiced by backers of Georgia.

The Trustees, upon whom the major responsibility for settling and governing the new colony rested, could receive no compensation for their work nor could they own land in Georgia. They spent much of their time, some of their money, and a great deal of effort in securing the necessary funds and the colonists, and in overseeing Georgia affairs during the twenty-year life of the Trust. The British Government carefully limited the powers of the Trustees. Any governor appointed or laws passed must be approved by the king, and royal instructions might be issued to all Georgia officials. Most of the work and the philanthropic interest, as well as the money to settle Georgia, came from the efforts of the Trustees. Imperial defense and control of foreign and Indian trade were reserved to the British Government. From such an arrangement the government could hardly help but profit, while its expenditures of effort or money would be little.

Once the Georgia charter was granted and the Trustees organized, the greatest propaganda campaign that preceded the founding of any American colony began. All England was aroused to the expected benefits to be derived from Georgia—philanthropic and humanitarian, imperial defense and expansion, and economic improvement. Contributions large and small were solicited by the Trustees and by many volunteer workers. Pamphlets were written and distributed, and sermons were preached. Gifts of money, religious tracts, and the seeds or roots of exotic but profitable plants were donated. The clergy of the Church of England were especially concerned. English Jews collected funds which they later used to send members of their own group to Georgia, contrary to the wishes of the Trustees. It was pointed out that Georgia could produce fine wines and relieve Britain of the necessity of importing Portuguese wines. She could supply hemp, flax, potash, silk, naval stores, spices of various sorts, and almost anything that was needed in Britain. She would relieve England of many poor and unfortunate and give them a chance for a new life. She could even take persecuted Protestants from other parts of Europe, especially Germans whose rulers happened to be Roman Catholic. Georgia could fill almost all the needs that any Englishman could suggest, if only Englishmen gave enough money to get her correctly launched.

In the selection of the colonists the philanthropic phase of Georgia's settlement predominated. The Trustees personally investigated every prospective settler who was to go at their expense—probably the most meticulous sifting process of any of the American colonies. Unfortunate but worthy people predominated in those selected to begin life anew in Georgia. The people who were to pay their own way were investigated along with any indentured servants they took to Georgia. Any debtor must first make an agreement with his creditor before he could be accepted. Apparently no one was accepted because he had been imprisoned for debt, and perhaps no more than a dozen Georgia colonists had ever seen the inside of a debtor's prison. Legend still makes the number much greater.

Oglethorpe accompanied the first colonists and helped to start the new colony. The original settlers, variously stated at from 114 to 125, sailed from Gravesend in November, 1732, in the frigate *Ann*. After temporary landings in South Carolina, where the colonists remained while Oglethorpe chose a site for the settlement, the entire body proceeded up the Savannah River and landed at Yamacraw Bluff on February 12, 1733. Here on a high sandy bluff overlooking the river, Savannah and Georgia were founded. An agreement for the land was made with the neighboring Indians, the Yamacraws, through their chieftain, Tomo-Chi-Chi. A few months later the Creeks ceded to Georgia all the lands between the Savannah and Altamaha rivers "as far as the tide ebbed and flowed."

Colonel William Bull and Oglethorpe laid out a neat and regular town, and the settlers began building their houses. Gifts of food and livestock from South Carolina were welcomed by Oglethorpe and the colonists. The Trustees had been so concerned with the spiritual and economic well-being of the colonists that little provision was made for government. Oglethorpe was a sort of agent of the Trustees and general overseer, but he had no specific title nor was there any political organization for the colony.

The first substantial non-British group to come to Georgia was one of German Protestants who were expelled from their home in the Archbishopric of Salzburg by their ecclesiastical prince. The first Salzburgers landed at Savannah in March,

1734, and were soon settled twenty-five miles upriver at a town which they called Ebenezer (Rock of Help). Further immigration brought their number to 1200 by 1741. The Salzburgers worked hard to transform the wilderness into a New Jerusalem and succeeded better than most early Georgians. The language barrier kept them apart from other colonists; and their close-knit social and political life centered in their church, whose ministers (John Martin Bolzius and Christian Rabenhorst) acquired considerable power. Their substantial brick church, easily the finest in colonial Georgia, is today a physical reminder of the faith and industry of these people who found religious liberty in the Georgia wilderness. Another group of German Protestants, Moravians, settled in Georgia from 1735 through 1738. However, a frontier province that needed defense against Indians and Spaniards was not the place for a people whose religious beliefs forbade fighting; so most of the Moravians soon left to join their brethren in Pennsylvania. In 1735, 150 Scotch Highlanders settled on the southern frontier at Darien, on the Altamaha River. Here the hearty Scots fought the Spanish and laid the foundations for economic prosperity.

Besides these main groups, Georgia soon had a sprinkling of people from Piedmont in Northern Italy, from Switzerland, and from Wales. A group of English Jews came in 1733. Charity colonists continued to be sent by the Trustees, and people who paid their own way came from England and a few from the other colonies. Additional settlements were founded near Savannah or in outlying areas. A fort was established by Oglethorpe at the falls of the Savannah River in 1735 to help Creek Indian relations. This fort and the town of Augusta, which grew up around it, soon became a center of the Creek trade and was of increasing importance throughout the colony's life.

EARLY DEVELOPMENT UNDER THE TRUSTEES

Upon his return to England in 1735, Oglethorpe took along his friend Tomo-Chi-Chi and several other Indians, whose presence in England did much to advertise Georgia. They were sufficiently impressed with England's magnificence, and the reports they brought back to America helped British-Indian relations in the Southern colonies. Oglethorpe returned to Georgia early in 1736 with two shiploads of new colonists, many of whom went to found the town of Frederica upon St. Simons Island, south of the Altamaha and the official limits of Georgia. Frederica, which soon became Oglethorpe's favorite Georgia residence, was always something of a military town where the martial spirit of Oglethorpe could have full sway. Other forts were founded along the inland passage and on the islands between Frederica and the St. Johns River, but there were usually insufficient troops available to garrison them.

When Oglethorpe returned to Georgia from his second visit to England in 1738, he brought back a newly raised regiment of troops and a commission as commander-in-chief of British forces in South Carolina and Georgia. Troubles between the English and the Spanish throughout the world were already pointing toward the war that was to begin the next year. Before it broke out, Oglethorpe negotiated a treaty, which the Spanish government refused to ratify, by which it was agreed that neither nation should occupy the mouth of the St. Johns River. At a 1739 meeting of Creeks, Cherokees, Choctaws, Chickasaws, and other Indians at Coweta Town, Oglethorpe improved Indian relations and induced the Indians to make a grant of all tideland between the Altamaha and St. Johns rivers. Upon his return from this trip, Oglethorpe learned that war had begun between England and Spain.

The Georgia-Florida frontier was but a minor battleground of this war, the War of Jenkins' Ear. Oglethorpe took the offensive as soon as possible and captured several Spanish frontier forts. In the spring of 1740 he set out with his regiment, Georgia and Carolina militia, and Indian allies to attack Florida. The attack did not go as planned, and the siege of the fort at St. Augustine was unsuccessful. Oglethorpe withdrew to St. Simons Island, where he was attacked two years later by the Spanish. After marches, counter marches, and skirmishes, the Spanish were defeated at the Battle of Bloody Marsh. This defeat plus a stratagem of Oglethorpe's frightened the Spanish into withdrawing from St. Simons and into abandoning any further attempt to capture Georgia. The next year Oglethorpe made another unsuccessful attempt to capture St. Augustine. This ended the War of Jenkins' Ear on the Georgia-Florida frontier. With the signing of a peace treaty in 1748, Georgia's immediate danger of Spanish attack was ended; and Oglethorpe's regiment was disbanded.

With no more battles to fight, Oglethorpe left Georgia for the last time in July, 1743. He had given ten of the best years of his life and a considerable portion of his fortune to the founding of the colony. He never received any compensation for his services in Georgia but did earn enduring fame. His interest in the colony continued throughout the life of the Trust, but it was not as intense as it had been heretofore.

The concern of the Trustees with the philanthropic aspects of Georgia's settlement led them to make several social and economic experiments. Each charity colonist was allowed fifty acres of land, five for house and garden in the town in which he lived and forty-five for farming outside the town. To prevent loss of land through bad management, it was granted for life and not in absolute ownership. To insure a fighting man for each fifty acres, lands could be held only by males. Georgia was to be settled in compact villages in an orderly progression, and not in the usual haphazard method of the frontier. Because charity colonists could not afford to buy slaves to work their acres, because Negroes could not help in the defense of Georgia, and because slavery would be a bad example where industry was to be encouraged—no slaves were allowed in the colony. Strong drink and lawsuits had helped to reduce some charity colonists to their unfortunate status. Hence there could be no strong drink—beer and wine excepted—and no lawyers in the colony. Such were the regulations set up in London; enforcement in Georgia was another matter.

A Trustees' garden was created at Savannah to receive all the plants that the mercantilists hoped Georgia would produce. Here the spices and other semi-tropical plants often died before they were transplanted to the fields of the colonists. Major emphasis was to be put on silk and wine. The Trustees put a design of silkworms into their common seal and brought over an expert from Northern Italy to instruct the colonists in silk production. All settlers had to plant a prescribed number of mulberry trees to furnish food for the silkworms. A filature was set up in Savannah to unwind the silk from the cocoons. While all early settlers were supposed to raise silk, the Salzburgers soon took the lead and raised considerable silk until Parliament cancelled the bounty upon its production in 1768. Henceforth silk production declined. Wine production met with less success from the start, and Georgians imported their own wine from Europe. Hemp had been produced in South Carolina with a colonial bounty, but lack of a bounty in Georgia rendered its production unprofitable.

In her early years, Georgia usually had to import some foodstuffs from South Carolina or the other colonies. The plantation system did not develop without slavery. The most profitable sources of income tended to be lumber products, cattle raising, and the Indian trade. Timber, barrel staves, and potash were forest products that found a ready market in the West Indies and in Europe. Large droves of cattle wandered through the woods and savannahs, were rounded up and branded at intervals, and were slaughtered and the meat salted for export, mainly to the West Indies. Augusta early became a rendezvous where Indian traders collected for shipment by river to Savannah the deerskins which formed the basis of the Southern Indian trade.

Most of the Trustees' utopian ideas for the improvement of human nature did not succeed. The prohibition against strong drink was the most unpopular and the hardest to enforce—in fact it was never really enforced. Rum was so universally drunk that juries would not convict for its sale. Trials by magistrates only were allowed in rum cases, but magistrates also liked rum and would not punish others for drinking it. Finally the Trustees decided to repeal their law against rum, but found technical difficulties in getting repeal approved by the British Government. After 1742 the law was simply ignored, and Georgians drank in peace so far as the law enforcement machinery of the colony was concerned.

The law against slavery fared no better. The industrious Salzburgers opposed slavery on economic grounds and the Scotch Highlanders on moral grounds, but other Georgians saw the "benefits" of slavery and wished for it, in order to escape labor in the hot sun. When the Trustees would not heed the demands for slavery, Georgians began to hire slaves from South Carolinians, and the practice continued until about 1750, when slavery was allowed in the colony.

Georgians wanted to own land in fee simple, and to be able to will or sell it to anyone they pleased. Many refused to plant the required number of mulberry trees or to work or improve land that might revert to the Trust. Complaints eventually led the Trustees to weaken the original land tenure regulation, which was really medieval and decidedly out of date, and finally abandon it altogether.

At the settlement of Georgia, the Trustees showed little concern for political matters, and never developed adequate government for the colony. The first government, in reality a town government for Savannah, consisted of a court presided over by bailiffs, assisted by constables. There was a secretary of the colony, in the person of William Stephens after 1737, a representative of the Trustees with no general powers. Ebenezer had a separate government of its own which was mainly dominated by its ministers and church elders. As long as Oglethorpe remained in Georgia, he was the government at Frederica and was often considered superior to the officials at Savannah; yet he was given no specific powers by the Trustees. After 1743 all Georgia was governed by a president and four assistants, resident in Savannah. They acted as a court of appeals from the local courts, but were representatives of the Trustees and not an executive body. The first elected assembly was called by the Trustees in 1751; but it had powers to recommend only, not to legislate.

Though something over 4000 people had come to Georgia, less than half of these as charity colonists, the population was considerably less than this during the period of the Spanish war, when Georgia reached its lowest ebb. Many of the colonists abandoned Georgia for South Carolina and the other colonies. With the removal of the Spanish danger and the restrictions of the Trustees, the population began to revive. By 1750 there were perhaps something over 2000 whites and 1000 Negroes in Georgia.

As would be expected in any philanthropic venture such as the founding of Georgia, organized religion played a large part. English churches and clergymen contributed money, Bibles, and religious tracts for the new colony, which became a favorite charity of many in the 1730's. A succession of Church of England clergymen came to minister to the spiritual needs of the colonists but often left the colony for personal or religious reasons with little accomplished. John and Charles Wesley were among this group but left more impress on the colony. Their colleague in early Methodism, George Whitefield, founded an orphanage and intended college, Bethesda, which was the best English school in the colony's early days.

After their usual custom, in 1751 the Trustees asked Parliament for an appropriation to help carry on the government in Georgia. But Parliament refused any further help, and the king declined to do anything for Georgia unless the Trustees surrendered their charter. The Trustees had wearied of their experiment in altruism and, having no further source of income, surrendered their charter and colony to George II on June 23, 1752, a year before their authority automatically expired.

The Trustees failed in most of their announced intentions in founding Georgia. No more than a dozen released debtors were ever sent to begin life anew, and most of the charity colonists showed that they were no better qualified to take care of themselves in Georgia than they had been in England. Furthermore, Georgia was not an outstanding success in the eyes of the mercantilists; few, if any, of the new items that it was supposed to produce were produced in appreciable quantities. In the race to get land before the Spanish, there was more success. From a standpoint of pounds and shillings, it can be argued that Georgia had cost more than it was worth. However, the Trustees had seen Georgia through its hardest years, and it would soon be able to grow and prosper under royal control.

A ROYAL COLONY

The royal government created in 1754 was similar to that of other royal colonies in America. There was a governor and council, a two-house assembly, and a court system. The main difference in royal government in Georgia and in the older colonies was that Georgia's principal colonial officials were paid from England. This gave them a certain independence of the colonial assembly that they did not possess in most other colonies where the assembly paid them. Georgians who owned fifty acres of land could vote for assemblymen. For the purpose of local government and church organization, Georgia was divided into eight parishes in 1758; and four more were added in 1765 for the lands south of the Altamaha. Parishes were no more than administrative areas; all real political power, local or provincial, was kept in the hands of the provincial government in Savannah.

Georgia's first royal governor, Captain John Reynolds, Royal Navy, arrived in 1754 and was recalled two years later after making himself eminently unpopular with Georgians by the use of quarter-deck methods even when they were clearly contrary to established forms of law. Reynolds was succeeded by an explorer and scientist, Henry Ellis, who was generally popular in Georgia and was a much more able governor than Reynolds. Ill health was responsible for Ellis' return to England in three years, before he could develop any long-range policies. In 1760 Georgia acquired her third and last royal governor, James Wright. Wright had served a colonial apprenticeship as attorney general of South Carolina and knew the workings of the London government from his term in London as South Carolina's provincial agent. His long tenure as Georgia's governor, his ability and interest in his job, and his personal interest in Georgia's development made him very influential in the development of the colony henceforth.

By 1763 Georgia had outgrown her peculiar traits of original colonization, had a well-organized and well-run provincial government, and had lost much of the danger of her frontier position. The Treaty of Paris of that year made Indian relations much easier than they had ever been before by removing the Spanish from Florida and the French from Louisiana. The Indian cession of all the lands between the Savannah and Ogeechee rivers as far as northwest of Augusta and of coastal lands between the Altamaha and the St. Mary's rivers made considerably more land available for settlement. Georgia's southern boundary was extended to the St. Mary's and made really definite for the first time. Across this new frontier was a friendly British province, East Florida.

Georgia's population grew rapidly after 1763, until at the outbreak of the Revolution it had between 40,000 and 50,000 people, almost half of whom were slaves. One of the first large groups to come to Georgia after the Trustees gave it up was a group of New England Puritans who had lived for several generations in South Carolina. They moved to Georgia in a body in 1752 and settled at Midway, St. John's Parish. In religion and local government they retained the Congregational forms and beliefs so common in New England. In material things they prospered, as was soon evident by their plantations and by the creation of their port Sunbury, as Georgia's second port of entry, in 1761.

A group of Germans under John Gerar William DeBrahm had settled at Bethany in 1751 and many more followed during the next few years. These, added to the Salzburgers, made Germans colonial Georgia's second most important national group after the British. Numerous Virginians and Carolinians arrived via the Appalachian valleys, especially in the last decade of the colonial period. In the late 1760's and 1770's many Scotch-Irish came from Ireland and settled at Queensborough on the Ogeechee River or on other parts of the frontier. Settlement was encouraged by the cession of lands north and west of Augusta by the Creeks and Cherokees in 1773. These lands were exceptionally fertile and were the best lands available to settlers in the Georgia-Carolina back country. Virginians and Carolinians poured into the 1773 cession at a rapid rate, and some groups of Scotch-Irish went directly there after arrival at Savannah.

By 1775 Georgia bore little resemblance to the utopia projected by the Trustees in 1732. Few, if any, of the original charity colonists remained. Strong drink and slaves were now legal and almost universal. There were enough lawyers in Savannah to be referred to collectively as "the bar." In the granting of land the limitations set up by the Trustees had long been forgotten. John Graham, Georgia's lieutenant governor and probably the largest land holder in the colony, held over 26,000 acres. Governor Wright had more than 19,000 acres and was probably the largest planter in the colony, with an estimated income of £6000 a year from his several well-cultivated plantations. He owned over 500 slaves. Rice on the coast and indigo and wheat farther inland were the main crops. Lumber products, naval stores, and deerskins were the contributions of the forests to Georgia's economy. Food and lumber products were exported to the West Indies; imports from there included slaves, sugar, molasses, and rum. Most of Georgia's manufactured goods came from England. Much food was brought from the northern colonies, but the upcountry settlement after 1773 helped production of provisions, especially flour and meat. The colony was following the general pattern of plantation economy common to the other southern colonies, but most Georgians were small farmers with holdings of 100 to 250 acres. The size of the land holdings was determined more by the newness of the area and the settlers than by any desire of the people or limitations of the government. Given time and peace after the Revolution, the plantation system would come into full flower in Georgia.

CHAPTER TWO

Georgia in the Revolution

T H E war between the American colonies and Britain that broke out in 1775 had its immediate cause in the new measures of colonial control adopted by the British government after 1763 and in the new and improved position of the colonies because the French menace was removed from North America in the same year. Most of the objections of the other colonies to restrictions on foreign trade and western land settlement did not have immediate application in Georgia, which had little foreign trade, almost no ship owners or importers, and had not nearly reached the limits of western settlement specified by the Proclamation of 1763. The removal of the French from Louisiana and of the Spanish from Florida, the rapid increase of population, and the settling of new lands after 1763 gave Georgians a new feeling of independence and self-sufficiency.

RISE OF DISCONTENT

The first item of Britain's new colonial policy that had any effect in Georgia was the revenue act known as the Sugar Act of 1764. While Massachusetts and other colonies were objecting to the act because it was a tax levied by Parliament, Georgia objected that new trade regulations would hurt her trade in lumber products with the West Indies.

The Georgia Assembly also objected to the Stamp Act passed in 1765 both because of the amount of the tax and because it was a tax imposed upon the colonies by Parliament. Georgians' objections, however, were not so strong as those in most colonies, and stamps were used in Georgia to clear vessels out of the harbor at Savannah—one of the few instances of the use of stamps in America. South Carolinians thought Georgia had acted so reluctantly in support of American liberty that they voted to stop all trade with Georgia.

Colonial rejoicing over the repeal of the Stamp Act in 1766 was stopped the next year by the passage of the Townshend Revenue Acts, which placed import duties on many items brought into the colonies from England. Soon the objections of the northern colonies to these acts were known in Georgia, and the 1768 assembly instructed Georgia's agent in London to work for their repeal.

In September there were several meetings in Savannah of "friends of liberty" and merchants, who decided to follow the plan used by other colonies and oppose the Townshend Acts by refusing to import British goods. Some orders to Britain may have been cancelled, but there was no agreement among Georgians as to a common policy. Certainly Georgia's objections were too little and too late to have any influence in London.

Although the Stamp Act and the Townshend Acts were the two biggest items over which Georgians and the royal government argued, they were not the only ones. The Commons House of Assembly objected strongly when Governor Wright refused to allow the election of representatives for the four new parishes south of the Altamaha River without specific instructions from England to do so and, in 1769 and 1770, refused to tax these parishes so long as they were not represented in the assembly. This argument ended in 1771 when royal instructions were received to allow representation of these parishes. There was a protracted argument between Wright and the Commons House in 1771 and 1772 over the right of the governor to disapprove a speaker chosen by the House. Two assemblies were dissolved because of their objection to such disapproval; but their chosen speaker, Noble W. Jones, did not serve. There were also arguments between the Commons House and the governor over furnishing supplies required by a Parliamentary act for troops stationed in the colony and about providing free passage for postmen on ferries under Parliamentary statute. In 1773 the Commons House appointed a committee of correspondence to communicate with the other colonies about American rights and problems, and thus Georgia went along with the other colonies in the American rights controversy.

Although many Georgians did not realize it and others did not want to face the fact, two schools of thought about relations with Britain were developing. Older inhabitants or recent arrivals from Britain tended to form a conservative group that generally went along with the British actions. A more radical group of people born in America who had few direct ties with Britain tended to insist upon American rights first, regardless of the British viewpoint. Noble Jones and James Habersham are good examples of the conservatives, while their sons (Noble W. Jones, James Habersham, Jr., and John Habersham) went along with the "American rights" group.

The first indication that some Georgians had really joined the revolutionary movement of the other colonies was the two meetings held at Tondee's Tavern in Savannah on July 27 and August 10, 1774, to consider the critical state of American affairs. The second meeting, which represented every parish, adopted eight resolutions condemning the actions of the British government and upholding the colonial opposition. It debated the selection of delegates to the First Continental Congress which was soon to meet, but did not select any. Leadership in both meetings came from a group of Savannah artisans, small business men, young men, and from the Puritans of St. John's Parish.

Opposition to these meetings, led by Governor Wright and his loyalist friends, made it obvious that many Georgians had not yet made up their minds to take sides for or against Britain. Deputies from four parishes met and elected Dr. Lyman Hall of St. John's Parish to represent them in the Continental Congress, but Hall refused to attend because the entire province had not acted. So the First Continental Congress met and adjourned with no delegate from Georgia present.

In January, 1775, the assembly met at the same time that delegates from five parishes held an unofficial meeting known as a provincial congress. This congress was designed to act for the entire province without the restraining hand of the governor. However, because it represented so small a part of the province, it acted as a sort of committee to prepare business which could be made official by the assembly. It adopted a non-importation agreement similar to the one just adopted by the Continental Congress and elected Noble W. Jones, Archibald Bulloch, and John Houstoun as delegates to the Second Continental Congress to meet in May. The assembly was badly divided, but when it showed a possibility of approving the action of the provincial congress, Governor Wright hastily prorogued it. Georgians were confused and far from united. The delegates to the Continental Congress refused to attend because they could not speak for the entire province. Apparently the non-importation agreement was ignored except in the parishes of St. John and St. Andrew. The radical party had made a valiant try, but it had not succeeded in taking Georgia all the way with the other colonies.

St. John's Parish, unable to take Georgia along with her in opposition to Britain, now tried to secede from Georgia and become a part of South Carolina, whence many of her inhabitants had come. South Carolina was sympathetic but refused to take on St. John's as a "detached" parish and would only recommend her to the Continental Congress. St. John's elected Lyman Hall to represent her in the Continental Congress and collected rice and cash to help Bostonians who suffered from the closing of their port by the British.

Throughout the first half of 1775, Georgians were steadily moving toward joining the other colonies in complete opposition to Britain. Mobs in Savannah and elsewhere openly flouted the customs laws and the authority of royal officials. In the parish of St. George courts were temporarily prevented from sitting. The Commons House of Assembly refused to convene in May at the call of the governor. The scheduled celebration of the King's Birthday was obstructed on June 4, and the birth of liberty was celebrated on June 5. Governor Wright said that he had no authority left and could accomplish nothing for the king.

In June and July there were a number of meetings in Savannah attended both by radicals and conservatives, but no compromise between them seemed possible. A June 22nd meeting elected Georgia's first council of safety or revolutionary executive body. A second provincial congress, representing ten of the twelve parishes, met on July 4. The parishes of Christ Church and St. John, the radical or Whig areas of Georgia,

dominated this congress and were able to obtain almost anything they desired. The congress moved rapidly to bring
Georgia in line with the other colonies. It ended trade with
Britain by adopting the Continental Association, approved all
action of the two Continental Congresses, and elected John
Houstoun, Archibald Bulloch, John J. Zubly, Noble W.
Jones, and Lyman Hall as delegates to the Second Continental Congress then in session. Its resolutions, the strongest that had
been adopted in Georgia, declared in plain terms that civil war
had begun in America, but expressed hope that compromise
might be possible. The congress provided for the election of a
successor and for a council of safety to carry on in the absence
of a congress. It was in effect Georgia's first revolutionary government. The council of safety, provincial congresses, and
local committees increasingly took over all governmental
functions. All effective power of the colonial government was
gone, but it continued to try to operate until Governor Wright
and other officials fled from Georgia in February, 1776.

On the surface there were perhaps as many reasons for
Georgians to remain loyal to Britain as there were to rebel. The
colony had received considerable financial help from England.
Many Georgians had been reared in England or had close
ties with her that they did not want to break. Colonial officials
and Anglican clergy worked for continued loyalty. Georgia's
only newspaper editor was a loyalist, but he did not let his
sentiments interfere with his journalism. Few Georgians were
personally concerned with the trade regulations so violently
objected to by the other colonies, and all saw the desirability of
the British army and Indian Department for protection
against the warlike Creeks.

Conversely, it should be pointed out that there were more
dissenters than Anglicans in Georgia and that there were few
Anglican clergy. The Scotch-Irish on the frontier, the High-
land Scots at Darien, and the New England Puritans at Midway
opposed many of the acts of the British government. From the
time of the Stamp Act there was a strong American Rights, or
Whig, Party in St. John's and Christ Church parishes. It was
influenced by other colonies and favored concerted action by
all. Many Georgians had come to consider themselves Ameri-

cans and did not want to be left out of any movement that
affected all of the colonies.

The desire of Georgians to regularize their new government
and the need for courts were responsible for the adoption on
April 15, 1776, of the first state constitution, a temporary
document called the Rules and Regulations. It consisted of
eight brief parts that created a government of three departments—legislative, executive, and judicial—with all power in
the hands of the legislative, still called a provincial congress.
The executive consisted of a president and a council of safety,
both elected by the provincial congress for a six months' term.
Archibald Bulloch, an early and consistent Whig leader, was
elected president. The new government made no change in
policy or machinery from that which had grown up unofficially
over the past eight months. Georgia was now in the hands of
the more radical Whigs, and no further talk of reconciliation
with Britain was heard.

Georgia's delegates to the Continental Congress were given
no specific instructions regarding independence, but they in-
terpreted their instructions of April 5, 1776, to work for the
common good of America as authority to vote for independence when it was considered. News of the Declaration of Independence, when received, was celebrated with appropriate
ceremony and joy in Savannah and throughout Georgia.

Georgia Whigs were excited early in 1777 by an attempt of
South Carolina to annex Georgia. The Carolina Assembly sent
William Henry Drayton to Georgia in January, 1777, to work
for a union of the two states. Drayton made a bombastic speech
to the assembly in which he pointed out the good that such a
union would bring about and the dire consequences to Georgia
if she did not agree to it. Button Gwinnett led the opposition to
this move, which apparently was opposed by most Georgians.
The assembly turned down the proposed union, and soon no
more was heard of it.

Once Georgia's Tories were silenced, the Whigs fell to arguing among themselves. The argument between radical and

conservative Whigs was intense, and finally erupted into a duel between Georgia's President Button Gwinnett and Colonel Lachlan McIntosh, leaders of the two factions respectively. Gwinnett died as a result of his wounds, and McIntosh was given an army command outside Georgia.

A new and permanent state constitution, adopted February 5, 1777, gave most political power to a one-house assembly that was apportioned roughly according to population. Executive powers were vested in a governor and executive council, both elected by the assembly. The court system consisted of a superior court for each county, made up of the state's chief justice and local assistant justices, and the existing local courts. Juries were to determine both fact and law. To take care of the physical growth, eight counties—Wilkes, Richmond, Burke, Effingham, Chatham, Liberty, Glynn, and Camden—replaced the colonial parishes. A bill of rights guaranteed equal division of property between heirs, free exercise of all religions, freedom of the press, trial by jury, and forbade entail and excessive fines or bail.

The constitution had simplicity of style and restricted itself to the barest fundamentals. It was entirely a Whig document, and most of its provisions can be traced to the eighteenth-century political philosophers and to colonial experience. It was one of the more democratic state constitutions written during the Revolution and put effective political power into the hands of the voters, who included almost the entire white male population. Political life under it continued much as in the colonial period except for the weakened executive and the new problems brought on by the war—especially the necessity of replacing the lost British trade, the purchase of needed military supplies, and confiscation of the property of Tories who remained loyal to the British.

Besides her political problems, Georgia also had military ones. Almost as soon as Georgians took over their own government, trouble developed with the British in East Florida. St. Augustine became the headquarters of the Tories from Georgia and the Carolinas, who raided south Georgia to get cattle and other food. In 1776, Georgia raised the battalion of troops authorized by the Continental Congress and felt that she was ready for action. From 1776 through 1778 an annual expedition of Continental troops, Georgia and South Carolina militia, and other military and naval forces set out to capture St. Augustine. There were always disputes among the commanders of the troops participating as to who should be the supreme commander; there was little cooperation among commanders; there was a lack of sufficient transport and supplies; and there were no well developed plans of action. The expeditions never got within striking distance of St. Augustine, and accomplished nothing except to illustrate how a successful military action should not be conducted.

SECOND PHASE: RETURN OF THE BRITISH

While a 1779 expedition against St. Augustine was being planned by the Whigs, the British decided to transfer their military operations to the South where it was thought that many Tories and Indians were ready to cooperate with them. At least 2000 British, loyalist, and German troops under Lieutenant Colonel Archibald Campbell were sent from New York in late 1778 to reconquer Georgia and, if possible, South Carolina.

Savannah was protected by General Robert Howe with Continental troops, by Georgia militia, and by the surrounding swamps. General Howe, Governor John Houstoun, and Colonel George Walton of the Georgia militia did not have sufficient liaison, and there was no single commander. After an unopposed landing on December 29, 1778, the British got into the town by an unguarded path through the swamps. A majority of the American troops were killed, wounded, drowned in the swamps in trying to escape, or captured by the British. A few Americans escaped into South Carolina, where Howe relinquished his command to General Benjamin Lincoln.

The British moved quickly to conquer all of Georgia. General Augustine Prevost led an expedition from St. Augustine to Savannah early in January, 1779, and Colonel Campbell occupied Augusta on January 31 with little Whig opposition. After their initial shock, Georgia Whigs in the back country began to collect militia, and General Lincoln gathered forces in South

Carolina to attack the British. Tory and Indian reinforcements did not flock to Campbell at Augusta. Instead Campbell withdrew upon the arrival of General John Ashe and some 1200 North Carolina troops. At the same time Whig militia under colonels Andrew Pickens, John Dooly, and Elijah Clarke defeated a group of 700 Tories at Kettle Creek in Wilkes County. Lincoln's plans to attack the British were disrupted when the troops under Ashe were defeated by the British at their camp on Briar Creek and the Savannah River on March 3.

A part of the British plan for the recapture of the southern provinces was to restore the civilian government as the first move in returning the area to its former colonial status. The British therefore invited all Georgians to resume their loyalty to the crown with no punishment for past opposition, and civilian government was restored. Georgia now had a provincial government in the British zone and a state government in the Whig zone with headquarters at Augusta. Governor Wright and other officials returned from England and resumed their old duties. Throughout the summer of 1779 Georgia remained divided between province and state, with no significant military action or change in the territory held by either side.

In September, 1779, Whig hopes were raised by the arrival of Count d'Estaing with a French fleet and about 4000 French troops. D'Estaing did not press his demand for the immediate surrender of Savannah, and the British were able to get 800 more troops into the town and to improve its defenses before d'Estaing and Lincoln began siege operations. D'Estaing soon found a siege too slow and stormed the British works on October 9. Many French and American lives were lost, but the defenses held. The French embarked and sailed away, and the Whigs were left without any hopes of regaining Savannah. Again it was the old story of "joint operations" without sufficient coordination between commanders.

After the success of the British at Savannah, Sir Henry Clinton brought an army from New York with which he captured Charleston, General Lincoln, and his entire army. In the summer of 1780 Augusta was occupied by the British, and many upcountrymen took the oath of allegiance to the king because they believed the Whig cause was dead in Georgia and South

Carolina. However, in back-country Wilkes County militia officers Elijah Clarke, Benjamin and William Few, and others continued guerrilla warfare against the Tories that developed such legendary reputations as those of Whig Nancy Hart and Tory Thomas Brown.

The provincial assemblies that the Governor called from 1780 through 1782 tried to repair the damages of the war years and to restore colonial government completely. All prominent Whigs were disqualified politically, and all actions of the state government were declared illegal. The British government contributed sufficient funds to the provincial government to make provincial taxes unnecessary, but the assembly did grant the king a 2½% duty on all exports produced in the colony as its share in imperial expenses. By late 1780 provincial officials and militia officers were appointed for all of Georgia, and Wright's government controlled most of it. But in 1781 the British began to lose control of the upcountry and continued to lose ground until in July, 1782, they evacuated Savannah.

If Governor Wright and the provincial government had troubles, the Georgia state government had considerably more in 1779 and 1780. The capture of Savannah in late December prevented the meeting of the new assembly in January, 1779. In January and July representatives of some of the counties met in Augusta and elected temporary executive councils that did what they could to keep state government in operation without claiming to be constitutional bodies. In November a group of the more radical Whigs proclaimed themselves an assembly, and elected George Walton governor; but the old executive council refused to recognize this government. For the last two months of 1779 Georgia had two Whig state governments and a provincial government in Savannah as well.

In January, 1780, an assembly met at Augusta and created one constitutional state government. This assembly, free of coastal domination, moved the capital to Augusta and provided for the development of the upcountry. Lands were made available easily in order to attract new settlers. In spite of such an encouraging beginning at restoring state government, British control of most of upper Georgia in the summer of 1780 put the existence of a state government in doubt for some months. The governor left, there were no elections, and no legislature met until August, 1781.

THE END OF THE REVOLUTION
AND ITS RESULTS

In the spring of 1781 the American Continental commander in the South, Nathanael Greene, began an offensive against the British in the back country. Augusta fell to the Whigs on June 5, and the British evacuated Ninety Six, South Carolina, on July 3. A Georgia Assembly met, elected Nathan Brownson governor, instituted a state government, and took steps to regain the loyalty of Georgians who had accepted British rule and to recall those who had fled to the North. Only Savannah and the immediate surrounding territory were held by the British. Whig refugees returned to the state. But there was still Whig-Tory guerrilla warfare in the no-man's-land between Whig and Tory Georgia.

General Anthony Wayne, Continental commander in Georgia, had trouble getting enough troops—Continental, state, or militia—to oppose the British. State troops formed out of ex-Tories who wished to reinstate their loyalty to the state often caused Wayne almost as much trouble as they did the British. Despite his inferiority in numbers, Wayne maintained an offensive that kept the British penned in Savannah. Because they had insufficient troops to hold both Georgia and South Carolina, the British evacuated Savannah in July, 1782, along with some 2000 to 2500 loyalists and 3500 to 5000 slaves.

The state government and American army moved into Savannah together, and one civil government controlled all of Georgia for the first time since 1778. The problem of protection against raids from East Florida continued throughout 1783, because its Tory population had been increased at the time of Georgia's evacuation. When the British evacuated East Florida in 1784 many of these Tories came back to Georgia to settle, generally with no major objections from Georgians.

One of the most controversial matters in Georgia in the immediate postwar years was the confiscation and banishment legislation against loyalists. The state confiscated all the property of those who had willingly sided with the British and banished such people. But, almost as soon as the last act was passed, the assembly began to mitigate its action. People named in the act had its penalties partially or completely removed or were required to turn over a part of their property to the state in lieu of confiscation and banishment. Many loyalists remained in Georgia or returned after a short absence. The state was anxious to enforce the act against only those who had considerable property or who had been particularly obnoxious to the Whigs. Perhaps a total of 1000 whites left Georgia permanently as a result of these acts.

While Georgians were concerned with "justice" to British sympathizers, they also desired to reward deserving Whigs. Land bounties were given to Continental and state troops, to militia, and to anyone who had helped with the war effort in Georgia, or elsewhere. Special grants were made to the higher officers who had served in the state, to injured veterans, and to the survivors of those who had lost their lives in combat.

The assembly sessions through 1785 were concerned mainly with the recovery from British occupation and the war years. Physical destruction had to be repaired. Those citizens who had left the state must be induced to return to Georgia, and new settlers encouraged. The legal confusion regarding property ownership, debts, and confiscation must be eliminated. Georgia must resume her proper relations with the Continental Congress, a matter which had been all but ignored since the British invasion.

During the war years, the state's expenses had increased considerably. No taxes were collected from 1778 through 1783, and expenses were generally met by the issuance of certificates of indebtedness or bills of credit. Confiscated Tory estates, from which it was hoped to pay the state's war expenses, were sold; but little promised in payment for them could be collected when it fell due. The state's indebtedness increased until 1785, but thereafter the amount owed to the state and the state's indebtedness began to be reduced. Most of the depreciated paper currency issued during the war was redeemed at a small fraction of its face value or repudiated entirely. Taxes remained low, but current expenses were met.

Just as soon as the fighting stopped, Georgia's economic progress, which had been slowed by the war, began anew. People coming into the state and taking up lands on the frontier increased its population, wealth, and military security. Merchants reported business good after 1783. Most of Georgia's trade continued to be carried on with Charleston, the British West Indies, and the northern states. Imports were mainly plantation supplies, with increasing amounts of luxuries as prosperity increased. Exports were lumber products and naval stores, rice, and some tobacco.

In social affairs, as well as in economic, there were attempts in the immediate postwar years to "get back to normal" and to adjust to the changes growing out of the war—the removal of British influence and control, the increasing importance of the frontiersman, and the reinforced belief in the importance of the individual and of popularly controlled political and social institutions. The older church denominations lost their prestige and were soon superseded by the Methodist and Baptist, the denominations of the frontier. The new importance of the individual was illustrated in the founding of state-endowed county academies, and the issuance in 1785 of the first charter for a state university.

Besides ordinary governmental operations, the major post-war political problems concerned troubles with the Creek Indians which grew out of the attempt of white Georgians to secure more Creek lands, disputes with the United States and Spain about ownership of large amounts of western lands, argument with South Carolina over the common boundary, and the adoption of the United States Constitution of 1787 and a new state constitution in 1789 to bring Georgia's government into line with that of the United States.

The effect of the Revolution and the separation from Britain resulted in several important changes in Georgia. The hard fighting and the isolation of the war years convinced many Georgians that they could get along by themselves without help from the British or the United States, but few had any real desire to do so. The fact that many of the colonial upper class were Tories and had left Georgia made it easier for the common man to direct political and social trends. The ease with which good land could be acquired gave this political and social democracy a solid economic base. The Church of England lost its privileged position, and education received considerable backing from the government. Certainly this meant that privilege and aristocracy stood for less and that a chance for the common man to make himself felt had arrived. Though the prosperity of the next half century would help to develop a sizable wealthy class, it was a very fluid aristocracy; and the common man never lost his importance in Georgia. Without the war years and the separation from Britain all this would have come much slower than it did.

CHAPTER THREE

Ante-Bellum Georgia, 1785-1860

POLITICAL DEVELOPMENTS

T H E new federal and state constitutions brought changes in both the form and substance of government in Georgia. The state constitution of 1789 created a two-house legislature, abolished the executive council and gave the governor considerably more executive power than any state governor had before possessed, and gave the franchise to anyone who paid a tax. This constitution was replaced by another written in 1798 that, with only twenty-three amendments, remained the fundamental law of the state until the Civil War. It followed the general outline of the 1789 constitution but showed more trust of the legislature and executive by including less statutory material in the constitution itself. Property qualifications for voting were abolished but were retained for office holding.

Local self-government really came into existence in Georgia in the post-revolutionary years when the assembly gradually surrendered to the counties more and more powers. Control over roads and ferries, local taxation, oversight of county poor, and election of county officials were the first powers given to local governments. Town self-government was introduced into Georgia with the incorporation of Savannah in 1787.

Of more immediate concern to many Georgians than their form of government was the problem of Indian relations, especially the desire of the whites to secure more of the rich piedmont lands from the Indians. This problem became acute just as soon as the British left Georgia. After ten years of negotiations and near wars, the Creeks gave up the lands between the Ogeechee and Oconee rivers by the Treaty of New York in 1790. However, Indian troubles continued because neither Indians nor whites really wanted to live up to the treaty agreements. Although the federal government after 1789 was stronger and better able to help Georgia in her opposition to the Indians, it did not always use this power in the way that Georgians thought it should. In fact there was almost a continuous feud between the two governments until the last Indians left Georgia in the late 1830's. After the United States set up a system of Indian trading posts in 1796, relations with the Creeks improved and remained generally good until the War of 1812.

Not only was the land which Georgia claimed to the Mississippi River occupied by hostile Indians in league with Spain, but also part of her western land in dispute between the United States and Spain, located between 31 degrees and 32 degrees 28 minutes, was actually occupied by Spain until 1795. In that year Spain ceded her claims to the United States; the United States created the Territory of Mississippi and then renewed her attempts to secure a cession of all of Georgia's western territory. In 1802, when Georgia was deeply involved in the Yazoo land frauds, she finally ceded the desired western territory in exchange for a promise that the United States would remove the Indians from Georgia as soon as it could be done peaceably.

With the ending of the confusion of the Revolution, immigration into Georgia increased rapidly. The 1790 census showed 82,548 people, and that of 1800, a population of 162,686. Most of these new settlers went into the rich back country that had been secured from the Indians in 1773 and afterwards. As long as the more conservative coast maintained its influence, the state's government was slow in creating new counties. Between 1790 and 1800, however, thirteen new counties were created, and the political domination of the coast became a thing of the past.

Colonial Georgia had been remarkably free of land speculation on the grand scale that was practiced in some other colonies. In the post-revolutionary period land acquisition became much easier. Over 4000 bounty grants were given to veterans, and anyone who wanted to settle in Georgia could get from 200 to 1000 acres of land under the headright system. There was considerable speculation with bounty grants of veterans who did not come to Georgia to settle, but most of the other grants made in the 1780's were to *bona fide* settlers. In 1789 land granting was put into the hands of county officials, and the way was opened for wholesale corruption. Often actual surveys were not made and the grantees filled in fictitious boundary lines to suit their fancy. By 1796 warrants had been issued for over three times as much land as existed in the part of the state freed from Indian control. In one county about twenty times as much land as the county contained was granted.

Such land frauds, however, were soon dwarfed by the greatest fraud that Georgia was ever to know—the Yazoo grants, so named because a part of the lands concerned lay along the Yazoo River, a tributary of the Mississippi. In 1796 the state sold between 35,000,000 and 50,000,000 acres of her western lands to four companies of speculators for $500,000. Promises of large grants to legislators were used to get approval of the sale by the assembly, and a large reserve of land was set aside to be sold to Georgians at the same price the companies paid—apparently to quiet any objections from Georgia citizens. James Gunn, United States Senator from Georgia, was one of the chief lobbyists before the legislature.

No sooner had the bill been passed than a storm of protest arose in Georgia. Grand juries, groups of all types, and individuals objected. One enraged community drove its legislator out of the state because he had voted for the sale. James Jackson resigned from the United States Senate, returned to Georgia, and got elected to the assembly to oppose the sale. The next year a new assembly cancelled the sales and ordered every reference to them erased from the state records. In the presence of both houses of the assembly, the act and all records connected with the sale were consigned to the flames. The new constitution of 1798 forbade the sale of western lands until they had been laid off into counties and regularly opened to settlement, and declared the Yazoo Act forever null and void.

Before the rescinding act could be passed, some of the Yazoo lands had been sold by the original companies, and the new owners refused to take the refunds offered by the state. Suits over this land were one of the reasons that induced Georgia to cede her lands west of the Chattahoochee to the United States in 1802. For many years Yazoo was to plague the United States government, which now inherited Georgia's interest in the matter. The case of Fletcher v. Peck arose out of the Yazoo sales and induced Chief Justice John Marshall to rule in 1810 that a legislative act may be a contract when it bargains for a sale. Having gotten her fill of such huge land frauds, Georgia's land granting was henceforth better controlled and in more manageable-size plots than the Yazoo sales.

As did most Southerners and Westerners, Georgians early offered to back the United States in the War of 1812, hoping that the war would result in the acquisition of Florida—a sanctuary for runaway slaves and lawless whites and a center of Creek Indian opposition to Georgia—by the United States. Though the United States was interested in Florida, she repudiated all action taken by Georgians aimed at annexation of that trouble spot. During the war the Creek Indians, with British backing, caused increased trouble; and Georgia joined the United States in a campaign against them. As a result of this victory over the Creeks, Georgia received some pine barrens in the extreme southern part of the state instead of the rich lands in Middle Georgia that she so ardently desired.

Peace with Britain ended Georgia's fear of invasion and temporarily stopped Indian troubles, but Florida continued to cause trouble. The United States authorized several military expeditions to break up trouble spots just over the border from Georgia. In 1818 General Andrew Jackson led such an expedition into Florida and hanged two British subjects whom he accused of making trouble. The controversy arising from this action finally led Spain to cede Florida to the United States the next year and so ended the Georgia-Florida boundary troubles.

With the War of 1812 and the Florida troubles out of the way, Georgians could return to pushing their Indian frontier further westward. In disposing of the lands between the Oconee and Ocmulgee rivers, secured from the Creeks in 1802 and 1804, Georgia developed a new land distribution system to replace the old headright system used since colonial days. Lands were first divided into counties and then into plots of

202½ acres each. These were distributed free in a lottery in which each citizen of the state had one chance, unless he belonged to the favored groups—Revolutionary veterans or widows, heads of families, and the like—who got additional chances. People who secured land from lotteries might cultivate it themselves or sell it. Henceforth, all public lands in the state were distributed in similar lotteries, except that the gold lands in the northern part of the state were given out in forty-acre lots.

As long as good farm lands in Middle Georgia could be secured from the Indians, the creation of new counties indicated newly settled areas and population increases. From 1800 to 1809, fourteen new counties were created; from 1810 to 1819, nine; from 1820 to 1829, twenty-nine; and from 1830 to 1839, seventeen. Since by 1840 all lands had been secured from the Indians, additional county creation represented further growth of sparsely settled regions or political maneuvering. During the same four decades Georgia's population increased from 162,000 to 691,000, the largest increases coming between 1800 and 1810 and between 1820 and 1830. The most pronounced growth was westward through Creek lands until the end of the period when it turned northwestward through the Cherokee lands. The coast grew slowly, and much of southwest Georgia remained sparsely settled. The capital of the state moved north and west with the population: Augusta in 1785, Louisville in 1796, and Milledgeville in 1806, where it remained until after the Civil War. With the westward movement, new towns sprang up and flourished. Those advantageously located for transportation, industry, and trade retained continued importance. Macon was founded in 1823 and Columbus in 1828, both at the falls of rivers, which gave them transportation and industrial advantages.

Ever since her earliest days, Georgia had been troubled by her Indian neighbors and had been pushing them farther and farther west. Her early troubles with the Creeks, who held the rich lands in Middle Georgia, have been recounted. Many Georgians felt that the promise of the United States in 1802 to remove the Indians should soon end the state's Indian problem, but this was not the case. The Creeks held to their lands tenaciously; and, to Georgians, it often seemed that the United States sided with the Creeks. In truth, the United States was caught between her promise to Georgia to remove the Indians and her desire to protect the rights of the Indians. The process of gradual cessions from 1785 through 1804 carried the Indians from the Ogeechee River to the Ocmulgee River and satisfied Georgians temporarily. But after 1804 there were no new cessions in the central part of the state for seventeen years.

In the meantime, many Georgians decided that it was time for the United States to fulfill her promise of 1802 and remove the Indians, even if force should be necessary. Neither President James Monroe nor President John Quincy Adams was willing to use force, but a voluntary cession of the lands between the Ocmulgee and Flint rivers was secured in 1821. A party of Creeks now decided to make no further cessions, as the only way to prevent movement west of the Mississippi River.

Governor George M. Troup announced that he intended to get all Creek lands in Georgia, by force if necessary. Negotiations in 1825 resulted in the Treaty of Indian Springs by which the Lower Creeks gave up the rest of the Creek lands in Georgia. The Upper Creeks, however, refused to abide by this treaty, and President Adams disallowed it because he maintained it was not negotiated properly. Troup said that he would enforce the treaty by war if necessary. While he threatened, the United States rushed negotiation of new treaties by which the Creeks gave up all their lands. Many of Troup's political enemies insisted that his threats of war against the United States were political propaganda and that he had no intention of sending state troops against the United States soldiers. At any rate, the last Creek lands were secured in November, 1827, and Georgia was soon rid of the Creeks.

Once the Creeks were gone, Georgians redoubled their efforts to get rid of the Cherokees, who occupied the northwestern part of the state. This tribe, the most civilized of the Southern Indians, had become an agricultural people and, under the influence of missionaries who worked among them, had a high regard for education and Christianity. Sequoyah developed his Cherokee syllabary in 1825, and many

Cherokees became literate in their own language. A newspaper, the *Cherokee Phoenix*, was established at the capital of New Echota (near the future site of Calhoun, Georgia); and books were translated into Cherokee and published. A national constitution was adopted in 1827 and the real beginnings of a superior yet native civilization were obvious among the Cherokees. Although this progress might be applauded by the missionaries, many Georgians did not approve. It would be more difficult to get lands from a civilized agricultural people than from barbarous hunters. Because the Cherokees fought removal to the west even harder than the Creeks and because they had a real central government that must act before anything could be done, Georgia decided that it would be impossible to get voluntary agreement for removal. Hence the legislature followed the suggestion of former Governor Troup and, on December 20, 1828, voted to extend state laws over the part of the Cherokee Nation in Georgia. Two years later Georgia forbade the Cherokee government to function within the state any longer.

The Cherokees ignored the Georgia action, adopted a nonbelligerent defense, and sought legal protection from the United States Supreme Court. The court refused to restrain Georgia on the grounds that the Cherokee Nation was not a foreign nation and had no right to sue in the court (Cherokee Nation v. Georgia, 1831). The next year the court, in the suit of a missionary in the Cherokee Nation, declared that Georgia's laws were not applicable to the Cherokee Nation (Worcester v. Georgia, 1832). However, President Andrew Jackson refused to enforce Chief Justice Marshall's decision, and the missionaries remained in a Georgia prison until they accepted pardons proffered by Governor Wilson Lumpkin.

To further complicate the Georgia-Cherokee troubles, gold was discovered in the Cherokee Nation in the summer of 1829; and large numbers of lawless white gold-seekers flocked into the Nation. This made the need for law and order more imperative and influenced Georgia even more to assert her authority within the Nation. In 1831 Georgia ordered the Cherokee lands surveyed, and the next year she granted them to her citizens. Soon whites were appearing in the Cherokee country to claim their new lands from the Indians or the missionaries who already occupied them. In the middle 1830's several treaties of cession were negotiated by the United States and unauthorized Cherokee representatives. Finally, in 1838, most of the Indians who had not already gone west were rounded up by the United States Army and taken to Indian Territory. This effectively ended Georgia's Indian problem.

The need for protection against Indians had been one reason why the Georgia ratifying convention had adopted the new federal constitution unanimously after brief consideration in 1788. But this did not mean that the people of the state were Federalists. In fact, most of them soon came to follow the political ideas of Thomas Jefferson, but there was no major division of the people on national issues until the rise of the Whig Party in the 1830's. However, this did not mean that there was unanimity in local affairs. Far from it! There early developed in Georgia two factions. The first strong state political leader after the Revolution was James Jackson, whose following largely controlled state politics until his death in 1806. Jackson's followers then collected around William H. Crawford and George M. Troup and came to be known as the Troup Party. This group tended to be the aristocratic or planter party, made up of the Virginia migrants, and followed Troup in state politics and Crawford in federal affairs. The opposition, or Clark Party, was led by John Clark, son of Elijah, and tended to be the North Carolina migrants or small farmer group. However, the personal leadership of Troup and Clark was more important than any other factor in determining party following. Political control of the state alternated between these two groups.

With the removal of Clark to Florida and the rise of Indian troubles, tariff, and nullification about 1830, the two groups adopted the names of State Rights (Troup) and Union (Clark) parties. The State Rights Party generally followed John C. Calhoun in national affairs, while the Union Party followed Andrew Jackson. Both groups favored getting rid of the Indians and opposed a protective tariff; they differed chiefly in how to achieve these ends. In the nullification controversy, Augustine S. Clayton led the nullifers while John Forsyth led the opponents of both nullification and the tariff. John M. Berrien opposed Jackson, the tariff, and nullification and was condemned by many nullifers and anti-nullifers. Forsyth and his group favored the calling of a general constitutional convention to settle this argument by constitutional amendment. After the nullification controversy died down and the Whig Party arose on the national scene, Georgia State Rights men generally became Whigs, while Union men tended to become Democrats. Georgia now alternated between Democrats and Whigs in local politics, with the Democrats being more often victorious, until the slavery controversy killed the Whig Party.

ECONOMIC ACTIVITY

After this review of politics, it will be well to turn to economic affairs; for wealth and population were constantly increasing in ante-bellum Georgia. As long as the area of white settlement continued to expand, there was constant need of more and better transportation facilities. Rivers had furnished the first transportation into the interior and continued to be important well into the nineteenth century. To keep river channels open for navigation, maintenance was originally done by the people who lived along the streams. Next, improvement by private companies was tried, but about 1820 the state undertook this function herself and soon appropriated funds for most of the important rivers. The development of steam navigation greatly enhanced the value of rivers as highways of commerce, and by 1830 steamboats were plying all Georgia's rivers between the coast and the fall line.

During the 1820's Georgia also became interested in turnpike and canal construction. Turnpikes were built mainly with private funds, a few with federal funds, and still fewer with private and state funds combined. Besides the turnpikes, there were local roads, usually poorly maintained by the people living along them. The only important canal constructed in Georgia connected the Savannah and Ogeechee rivers, but was not finished until 1831 and was soon abandoned because of the coming of railroads. In the 1820's there was extensive planning, both public and private, of a comprehen-

sive system of canals or railways to link all parts of the state.
The state created a board of public works and employed a chief
engineer to consider a comprehensive plan, but abolished the
board the next year before it could accomplish anything.
Because Georgians had not responded very enthusiastically
to the building of canals and turnpikes, there was all the more
need for the development of railroads once they became practical. By 1833 the advantages of railroads became obvious
when one was built from Charleston to Augusta. In the same
year the Georgia Railroad was chartered to construct a road
between Augusta and Athens, a road which was finished in
1841. The Central of Georgia Railroad to join Savannah and
Macon was also begun in 1833. Its completion in 1843 joined
the state's main port to its richest farming area. A railroad
promotion convention in 1839 recommended that the state
build a railroad from the Chattahoochee River to the Tennessee state line. This road, the Western and Atlantic, was begun
the same year with state funds and completed in 1851. It was
operated by the state until after the Civil War. To join the state
road, both the earlier railroads extended their lines to its ter-
minus. The Georgia Railroad reached the Chattahoochee in
1845 and the Central of Georgia in 1846. At this junction an
important transportation center, Atlanta, grew up. Connections with the west were secured when the Atlanta and West
Point Railroad began a route to the Alabama state line in 1845.
Independent short lines and branch lines were built, so that by
1860 Georgia had 1226 miles of railroad that covered well the
central part of the state and extended into the northwestern
and southern extremities.

The greatest need for a transportation system was to serve
agriculture and the forest industries, from which the great
majority of Georgians earned their livelihood. Though Georgia was a plantation state, the unit was the farm rather than the
plantation for at least two-thirds of her land and for even more
of her people. By 1860 there were in Georgia 902 plantations
of more than 1000 acres (206 more than in any other state);
2662 of from 500 to 1000 acres; 18,823 farms of from 100 to
500 acres; and 31,000 of less than 100 acres. Ownership of
twenty slaves, often taken as the dividing line between planters

and farmers, was true in the case of 6363 Georgians. Thus the majority of the people were yeomen farmers who owned only a few slaves, if any. In fact, something over three-fifths of Georgia's families owned no slaves at all. The poorest yeomen owned no slaves and generally had no outside labor on their farms. Below the yeomen farmers in the economic and social scale were the poor whites, often contemptuously referred to as "poor white trash," who cultivated a few acres to produce the necessary food and spent much time in idleness. There were no hard and fast lines between these three groups, and movement from one to the other was easy for the competent, the industrious, or the lazy. Neither was there any geographic separation of the groups, but the poorer whites tended to congregate on the inferior lands in the mountains or the pine barrens in the southern part of the state.

Georgia's main cash crops, from plantation or farm, were rice and cotton. Rice and sea-island cotton were raised on plantations near the coast. More money was made from upland, or short staple, cotton, which was raised throughout the central part of the state by planters and farmers. By 1825, Georgia led the world in cotton production, with 150,000 bales annually. The average plantation also produced a large percentage of the food consumed by man and beast. The ordinary yeoman farmer produced all his food and some surplus for sale as well as a staple money crop. More acreage was probably planted to corn, mainly for local consumption, than any other crop. Small grains, sweet potatoes, and tobacco were also important as money crops or for local consumption. Certainly farmers had sufficient food, though the diet might not have been well balanced according to present-day standards.

There was in ante-bellum Georgia little of what could be called scientific farming. A state agricultural society, various local societies, and some planters introduced new crops or farming methods. In 1854, the University of Georgia set up a department of agriculture, using a gift made for that purpose. However, the average farmer seldom thought the new discoveries were practical on his farm or bothered to learn about them. To teach slaves new methods took more supervision than many planters or overseers cared to exert. Consequently, the amount of agricultural improvement that took place was not very great. Usually new crops and new methods resulted from low prices for the old crops or methods, and a rise in prices would often end any experimentation. The availability of good cheap land made it unnecessary for the average farmer or planter to be concerned with better agricultural methods. When new lands disappeared in the 1840's, there was some increased interest in better farming methods.

Many of Georgia's farming methods continued to be geared to the Negro slaves who furnished plantation labor. Georgia had discontinued the foreign and domestic slave trade before 1800, but reopened the domestic trade in 1824. Illegal importation of slaves from Africa continued until the very eve of the Civil War. The attitude of the late eighteenth century that slavery should and would be discontinued disappeared by the 1830's because of the increased economic value of slaves, the inability to find a solution to the problem of what to do with freed slaves, and the slackening of the idealism that had accompanied the Revolution. There was a general feeling that free Negroes were undesirable. They were not citizens, and they were hedged about with numerous special restrictions that made their lot little better than slaves. Yet by 1860 about one percent of Georgia's Negro population was free. Education of free Negroes and slaves was forbidden by law, but this law and many others that sought to limit the activities of Negroes were often violated with impunity by whites who approved the laws in theory but thought that exception should be made for the Negro concerned.

Georgians were interested in manufacturing as well as in agriculture. During the Revolution and the War of 1812 the state government tried to encourage manufacturing, without much success. Once the impact of the cotton gin was felt, the raising of cotton rather than its manufacture became the matter of first concern to most Georgians. Home or village industry was carried on, but few factories existed until the 1830's when some cotton and woolen textile mills were founded, mainly along the fall line where water power was available. Manufacturing developed slowly because of the lack of sufficient capital, the lack of an adequate source of good labor, and the general feeling that more money could be made in agriculture than in manufacturing. However, by 1850 Georgia had forty cotton mills and was one of the leading producers of cotton textiles in the South. In addition to cotton mills, there were also tanneries, shoe factories, iron foundries, machine shops, nail factories, and brick and pottery works. By 1860, there were 1890 manufacturing establishments of all sorts, employing 11,575 laborers, and producing goods valued at $16,925,564. But most Georgians still got their support directly from the land.

Cotton, being the greatest item of agricultural and industrial production, was also the largest item in Georgia's trade. Because of cheap water transportation, the fall line cities became the first cotton markets and retained their supremacy after the coming of railroads. The sale of other staple crops usually followed the same pattern as did that of cotton. Corn and foods were most often sold locally and were not exported. Manufactures from the northern states and Europe made up the greatest amount of imports into Georgia. They were often imported and sold by the same merchants who bought and exported cotton.

As business and agriculture grew, more capital was needed, and banks were founded to help supply this need. During the 1820's, when banking was new to Georgia, the state government invested considerable money in bank stocks, operated a bank in connection with its treasury, and actually anticipated a time when profits from banking would eliminate taxes. But with the hard times of the 1830's and many bank failures, it soon became obvious that taxes would continue for some years to come.

Generally the decade of the 1850's was a prosperous one in Georgia and the South. Agriculture, especially cotton production, flourished and so did manufacturing and trade. Many Southerners were sure that prosperity had come to stay and that their economy was really considerably superior to that of the northern states, which seemed more subject to economic depressions.

SOCIAL AND INTELLECTUAL CONDITIONS

Before the Civil War, Georgians did not try to live by cotton alone, but were also interested in education, religion, and other cultural matters. Georgia had begun her life as an independent state by declaring that education should be a public charge, and had created a system of state-endowed county academies in the 1780's. But this early interest in education was not continued throughout the ante-bellum period. After the creation of these academies, they were left without further state support. Georgia's next step in the support of elementary education came in 1817 when she set aside a poor-school fund of $250,000, increased to $750,000 in 1821. From this fund the state agreed to pay for three years' education in reading, writing, and arithmetic for the children of the poor. Many parents did not avail themselves of even this small amount of education for their children, for in 1850 twenty percent of adult white Georgians were illiterate. Most counties did nothing to supplement the poor-school fund, but a few actually set up public school systems which furnished free education to the children of all citizens.

Between 1836 and 1840, with a part of the money distributed to the states by the federal government, Georgia provided for increased state school funds which should establish free schools for all children. The plan, however, was apparently too bold, because it was cancelled in 1840 and the old poor-school system restored. No further consideration of the state's educational needs and demands for improvement was made until 1858 when the legislature again provided for the establishment of a free public school system. Before this system could begin operation, the Civil War intervened.

The University of Georgia, chartered and endowed with land in 1785, began operation in 1801. Its curriculum soon lost the scientific trend given it by the first president, Josiah Meigs, and became primarily classical. After the original endowment of the University, the state ignored its monetary needs. In 1821 the University sold its landed endowment and loaned the proceeds to the state, for which it received $8000 annual interest, its only sure source of income throughout the ante-bellum period. In spite of such hardships, the University occupied an important place in the life of the state; and most of Georgia's leaders, especially in politics, were educated in Athens. Luckily, Georgians were not dependent entirely upon the support of their state government for education. Private schools of varying worth flourished, and some children were sent out of the state to be educated. Clergymen supplemented their incomes from teaching, and the desire of the religious denominations for a trained clergy led to the founding of religious schools and colleges. Georgia's religious schools were often a combination of manual labor and classical so that poor youth might receive the advantages of education. In the 1830's the three leading denominations each set up a college: the Methodists founded Emory at Oxford; the Baptists, Mercer at Penfield; and the Presbyterians, Oglethorpe near Milledgeville. In 1843, the Methodists secured control of Georgia Female College in Macon and renamed it Wesleyan College, the first school to offer college work for women in the state and one of the first in the nation. In addition to these schools, there were in 1860 over forty institutions calling themselves colleges, about half of them with some religious connection. Most of these were really secondary schools, rather than colleges.

Professional societies advocated better training methods in their fields and otherwise helped to improve their professions. The Georgia Medical Society was founded in Savannah in 1804 and was soon followed by local societies in other cities. The first medical college in the state, founded at Augusta in 1828, received financial support from the local medical society, the city, and the state. Medical colleges were founded in other cities, especially Savannah and Atlanta in the 1850's; but the Augusta college remained the outstanding one in the state.

Those aspiring to be lawyers continued to read law in some law office, until 1859, when Georgia's first law school was founded in Athens by Joseph Henry Lumpkin and Thomas R. R. Cobb, leading attorneys. It was connected with the University of Georgia from the first, but did not become an integral part of it until after the Civil War. A military school was founded in Marietta, with some public support, in 1851, and a business college in Atlanta in 1858.

The democratizing influence of the Revolution made itself felt in the churches as well as in education. The leading denominations of the colonial period—Episcopal, Lutheran, and Presbyterian—had been formal in their worship and intellectual in their appeal. These churches lost ground; and the democratic frontier churches with an emotional appeal, especially the Methodist and the Baptist, became the leading denominations. Slaves were usually associated, formally or informally, with the denomination of their masters.

Despite the work of local circuit riders and visiting evangelists, only ten percent of Georgians claimed any church affiliation in 1831. Church membership increased considerably throughout the 1840's and 1850's, especially after the formation of Southern church organizations in the 1840's. Camp meetings were part of the religious picture throughout the ante-bellum period and brought many into the church. In 1860 there were 2393 churches in Georgia, distributed as follows: Baptist, 1141; Methodist, 1035; Presbyterian, 125; Union, 27; Episcopal, 25; Christian, 15; Lutheran, 9; Catholic, 8; Cumberland Presbyterian, 4; Universalist, 3; and Jewish, 1.

In addition to its support of churches, any Christian community has to take care of its unfortunates, and ante-bellum Georgia was concerned with them. The oldest philanthropic organization in the state was the Union Society, founded in colonial Savannah, which helped to educate and support orphans and other unfortunates. Orphanages were founded, usually with the backing of religious denominations. Many orphans were apprenticed to tradesmen or farmers. In 1837 the state founded an insane asylum at Milledgeville, and began care of the mentally deficient. Ten years later, responsibility for the education of the deaf and dumb was assumed, with the founding of a school at Cave Springs. In 1852 the academy for the blind at Macon became a state institution. After the beliefs of the day, Georgia was doing as much as could be asked in taking care of these unfortunates.

Another group of unfortunates of a different type consisted of those people who had broken the law and were imprisoned. There were numerous Georgians who believed that criminals should be reformed rather than merely punished. This belief led to the creation of a penitentiary at Milledgeville in 1817, where reform would be easier than in isolated county jails. Here convicts were set to work on useful tasks, usually some type of manufacturing; but they never produced enough to pay for the system as some had argued that they would. Undoubtedly the prisoners got better treatment in the penitentiary than in local jails, and some were taught a useful trade and reformed. The state several times revised its criminal law and removed or lightened many of the harsh punishments inherited from an earlier period. One reform, which came in 1823, was the abolition of imprisonment for debt.

The treatment of its unfortunates and criminals is hardly the real measure of a civilization. Interest in and production of literature is a better sign of cultural level, and in this Georgia did not rate very high. Before the 1830's she was too much a frontier state to be concerned with literary matters, and after that she was too much concerned with economics, politics, and the slavery controversy. Books continued to be imported from Europe and the North, but libraries increased in number and size. Most of the libraries of the period belonged to private societies which were supported by membership dues. There were numerous other societies which aimed at cultural and social improvement: debating societies, societies for the diffusion of knowledge, societies for the improvement of morals and correction of vices, societies for benevolent and social purposes, and societies of artisans that performed the social and benevolent duties of modern labor unions. Savannah and Augusta had theaters throughout most of this period, and a few existed in other cities by 1860. There were also entertainments presented by local societies, traveling actors, musicians, jugglers, and the like. Lecturers strove to improve knowledge and morals and to give more elegance to social life. But most Georgians preferred barbecues, horse races, dances, lodge meetings, political rallies, court days, militia musters, and camp meetings for their social activities.

So far as literary production in Georgia was concerned, history and literary humor led. Edward Langworthy, who participated in the political and military happenings of the Revolution, intended to write a history of that period but never did. Hugh McCall published in 1811 and 1816 his *History of Georgia,* the first work to cover the colonial and revolutionary periods; but he did not do a really adequate job. Georgia's centennial in 1833 brought about a renewed interest in history, the founding of the Georgia Historical Society in 1839, and the state government's sending to England to have Georgia's colonial and revolutionary records copied. With the encouragement of the Historical Society and the use of the recently copied records, William B. Stevens, a clergyman and faculty member at the University of Georgia, published in 1847 and 1859 the first really adequate history of colonial and revolutionary Georgia. George White published two volumes of historical records in the 1840's and 50's, and Adiel Sherwood published a *Gazetteer* in 1827 and 1832.

There are several writers of fiction in ante-bellum Georgia worthy of mention. Francis R. Goulding's *Young Marooners* is an adventure story, popular from its first appearance. But the two best-known literary producers of the period were humorous writers. Augustus Baldwin Longstreet recorded humor and frontier social history in his *Georgia Scenes,* and William Tappan Thompson carried forward the same tradition in *Major Jones's Courtship.* In poetry Thomas Holly Chivers' erratic genius attracted attention, and Richard Henry Wilde's "My Life is Like the Summer Rose" is noted for its melodic beauty as well as the controversy about its authorship.

If few Georgians were interested in history or literary works of merit, many more were interested in the newspapers, especially during political campaigns when a fearless brand of personal journalism was engaged in. Georgia newspapers grew in number, size, and circulation. The leading ones were published in Savannah, Augusta, Columbus, Athens, Milledgeville, and Macon. There was to be found in Georgia a journal that favored almost any political idea, until the rise of the slavery controversy. However, no abolitionist newspapers were ever to be found in Georgia. There was also an active religious periodical press, the most popular member of which was the Baptist *Christian Index,* founded in 1821 and still being published today. There were agricultural periodicals (the *Southern Cultivator* was founded in 1842), literary and semi-popular periodicals, and a few professional journals. The interest in "Southern" newspapers, periodicals, and books was helped by the rise of the slavery controversy and the desire of Georgians to have reading material produced at home and uncontaminated by abolitionist ideas.

It was during the period 1790–1860 that Georgia matured physically, economically, socially, and culturally. The Indian population was replaced with whites and Negro slaves. Colonial and Revolutionary Georgia had been very conscious of the fact that it needed outside military help. By the time of the Creek and Cherokee troubles in the 1820's and 1830's, Georgians were certain that they could take care of themselves and even threatened to fight the United States government itself when it seemed to side with the Indians. With the spread of cotton culture throughout the central counties, the state was in a better economic position than she had ever been before and was able to support herself adequately. Politically, Georgians had been sure that they were able to take care of themselves since the late colonial period. Culturally and socially, with the passing of the frontier, there was the progress that comes with maturity. In short, Georgia lost the traits of her peculiar infancy, ceased being a frontier area, and became an integral part of the Southeast, similar in most respects to the other cotton states.

CHAPTER FOUR

Slavery, Secession, and the Civil War

SLAVERY AND THE SECTIONAL STRUGGLE

S L A V E R Y was a problem in Georgia from the founding of the colony. Originally the colonists objected because they were not allowed to own slaves. After slavery was allowed, there were objections on both moral and practical grounds and a general feeling at the time of the Revolution that slavery was wrong and should be ended soon. However, the waning of the idealism of the revolutionary generation, the invention of the cotton gin, and the inability to find a satisfactory solution to the problem of what to do with the freed slaves all resulted in a steady increase in the number of slaves and less concern about ending slavery. In fact, by the 1830's most Georgians had ceased to consider slavery an evil, many had come to consider it a positive good to both Negroes and whites, and most were willing to go along with the law that made it illegal for freed Negroes to remain in the state.

Georgians, like most other people in the United States, were surprised at the troubles that arose over the question of slavery in the territories, a problem which was temporarily settled by the Missouri Compromise of 1820. Once the slavery controversy had been brought up, it remained a touchy question upon which Georgians could always be aroused. They reserved their choicest epithets for William Lloyd Garrison and abolitionists of his type, and even offered rewards for the capture of Garrison (safe in New England) or his associates.

By the time enough people from the Southern states had settled in Texas to make its status a point of interest to the United States, it became involved in the slavery controversy. Georgians were sympathetic with Texans, many of whom had come from Georgia originally. When Texas revolted against

Mexico in 1835 and then wanted to be annexed to the United States, Georgians generally approved the Mexican War and furnished the troops requested to fight it, but such prominent Georgians as Whig Congressman Alexander H. Stephens and Senator John M. Berrien opposed both the annexation of Texas and the Mexican War. However, once the war was fought, practically all Georgians (including Stephens) opposed the Wilmot Proviso, which would exclude slavery from the newly acquired territory.

The necessity of establishing a government for this territory, the application of California for admission as a free state, and the demand of Southerners for a new fugitive slave law produced a crisis in 1850. A Georgia triumvirate of Alexander H. Stephens, Robert Toombs, and Speaker Howell Cobb joined Henry Clay, Daniel Webster, and others in backing the Congressional Compromise of 1850. Stephens, Toombs, and Cobb returned to Georgia and stumped the state in favor of the Compromise and were able to get considerable backing. Conservative Georgians dominated a state convention that met in December, 1850, and adopted the "Georgia Platform." This platform recognized that the Compromise of 1850 did not secure all that the South demanded but, because it preserved the Union, urged acceptance by the South as the best solution of the immediate problems before the country. The nation was warned that it must live up to the Compromise fully to save the Union, for the South would surrender no more of its demands. This Georgia Platform became the rallying cry of Southern unionists to oppose disruption of the Union, an idea put forward by South Carolina radicals in a convention attended by most Southern states at Nashville the same year.

The Georgia Platform had been the work of Whigs, led by Toombs and Stephens, and Democrats, led by Howell Cobb, and was responsible for a new political alignment in Georgia. Those who favored the Compromise of 1850 called themselves the Constitutional Union Party and elected Cobb governor in 1851. Those who opposed the Compromise adopted the name Southern Rights Party. These new parties resulted from a marriage of necessity when neither of the old parties adequately fulfilled the immediate political needs of the state. This marriage, however, was short-lived, breaking up during the presidential election of 1852, when Whigs and Democrats reverted to their respective parties. By 1854 the Whig Party was dead in Georgia; most of its leaders became Democrats, except a few such as Benjamin H. Hill and Eugenius A. Nisbet, who went into the Know-Nothing Party.

Georgians approved Douglas' Kansas-Nebraska Bill of 1854 and provided money and free transportation over the state railroad to encourage slave-state emigrants going to Kansas. Few, however, went from Georgia. Of more interest to Georgians was their own gubernatorial election of 1857. When the Democratic convention found itself confronted with too many candidates, it nominated a dark horse, Joseph E. Brown, a yeoman farmer and judge from North Georgia. Georgians soon discovered Brown to be a man of considerable ability with determination to do what he considered right. He was a strong states-rights man; but, what was more important at first, a very able state executive. He eliminated poor business methods in state government, greatly increased the income from the state railroad, and made himself felt as a strong governor and friend of the common man. In many respects, Joe Brown was the Andrew Jackson of Georgia; and his election gave the common man a feeling of being more a part of the government than he had felt before.

SECESSION

Georgians soon turned from state politics to the more troubled national scene, especially the split in the Democratic National Convention of 1860 over Stephen A. Douglas' popular sovereignty in the territories. When the convention refused to advocate protection of slavery in all the territories, the Georgia delegates joined other Southerners in withdrawing. Two new Democratic Conventions resulted from this split, and a Georgia delegation participated in the convention that nominated John C. Breckinridge on a slavery extension platform. The state's vote was split between Breckinridge (51,893) and John Bell (42,855) of the Constitutional Union Party, despite the fact that the Douglas ticket carried a Georgian, Herschel V.

Johnson, in its second place. As no candidate received a majority of the votes cast, the legislature chose the electors, giving the state's vote to Breckinridge.

With the election of Lincoln many Southerners felt that they must act before it was too late. While most Southerners believed in the constitutional right of secession, there was a difference of opinion as to how it should be effected or whether secession was necessary. One group maintained that the Southern states should come out of the Union at once. Another group insisted that a convention of all the slave states should meet and decide upon a common course of action. The group in favor of immediate action succeeded in carrying the day, and individual state conventions were called. On December 20, 1860, South Carolina seceded from the Union.

Georgia and the other slave states must now decide their course of action. Governor Brown, Robert Toombs, Thomas R. R. Cobb, and distinguished visitors from out of the state urged the legislature to call a secession convention at once. Alexander H. Stephens raised almost a lone voice insisting that a Republican president with a Democratic Congress could not hurt slavery and that the South should wait and see what Lincoln would do rather than destroy the union without any real provocation. Instead, he argued, all Southern states should act together. The legislature called a convention to meet in January, appropriated $1,000,000 for defense, and authorized the raising of 10,000 state troops.

In the election to Georgia's convention the vote was 50,243 for candidates favoring immediate secession and 37,123 for those who opposed such action. Secession feeling was strongest in the cities and the plantation section of the state, while unionist strength lay in the mountains and pine barrens. In the convention which met from January 16 through 29, 1861, Benjamin H. Hill and Herschel V. Johnson joined Stephens in opposing immediate secession, but they made no headway. The failure of any of the compromise efforts tried both in Congress and outside and the growing belief that the South could bargain better outside the Union than inside increased the strength of those favoring immediate secession. On all crucial issues, the convention divided about 165 to 130 until the

final vote for the ordinance of secession, which was 208 to 89.
The convention, having made Georgia an independent nation,
retained all United States laws, regulations, and officials, with
certain minor changes. It appointed delegates to the convention of the other seceding states soon to meet in Montgomery,
Alabama, to organize the Southern Confederacy.

In Montgomery, Georgia delegates took a lead. Howell Cobb
was elected president of the convention, Thomas R. R. Cobb
was a leader in the writing of the Confederate Constitution,
and Robert Toombs was prominently mentioned for president. In the end, Jefferson Davis was selected as president, and
Georgia was represented in the new government by Alexander
H. Stephens as vice president and Robert Toombs as secretary
of state. A new state constitution was now adopted, but it made
few changes in Georgia's fundamental law.

When it became obvious that the Confederate States were
not going to be allowed to leave the Union peacefully, they
began to prepare for war. After Lincoln issued his call for
75,000 volunteers on April 15, 1861, Georgians began to offer
their services to the state or to the Confederacy. In June, military units were being raised by the state, and 18,000 volunteers
were reported organized and ready for service. The 22,714
stands of arms taken from United States installations in Georgia were turned over to the Confederacy. All available weapons
were collected and repaired, but few new ones could be secured. Soon there were more volunteers than could be armed.
Governor Brown tried to solve this shortage by refusing to
allow any Georgia troops to carry their arms out of the state
when they departed for the Virginia front. Money was appropriated to purchase arms, orders were placed in the Confederacy and in Europe, and by 1862 a factory capable of producing
125 rifles a month had been established at the state penitentiary. Neither the state nor the Confederacy ever solved its
arms supply problem, even though Governor Brown tried the
expedient of arming some troops with pikes, which were considerably easier to manufacture than rifles.

Once the initial supplies of cloth and clothing were
exhausted, military and civilian shortages developed. Home
and factory manufacture was urged, and considerable conser-

vation and rehabilitation of clothing were carried on during the war. With the possible exception of shoes, clothing was easier to manufacture than armaments. The greatest shortage was in wool and woolen cloth. Medicine and hospital supplies were soon in short supply, with little prospect of securing needed amounts. Georgians collected such supplies as were available, produced what herbs and medicines they could, made bandages and hospital clothing, and sent whatever they had to Virginia for use by Georgia troops. Rest houses were set up near railway stations to care for the needs of and provide comforts for soldiers going to or returning from the front.

POLITICS DURING THE WAR

By the time of the 1861 state elections, there were suggestions that politics be adjourned for the duration of the war; but this did not happen. In 1861 and 1863, Governor Brown was re-elected for a third and a fourth term, despite the fact that no Georgia governor had ever served three terms before. In neither of these elections did Brown make a formal canvass; instead, he gave out letters and printed statements. In each election he was opposed by the majority of the state press, on the grounds that he was dictatorial, that he did not agree sufficiently with the Davis administration, and that he had been in office too long already.

Brown continued his bold type of politics in which he did what he thought was best, regardless of the opposition of the Confederate administration or of Georgia critics. At times he pursued rather unpopular policies, such as the seizure of salt and other scarce provisions and his opposition to the distillation of liquors. Brown's enemies always predicted that he had gone too far and that some specific action would cause his political death, yet the great mass of the common people always rallied to his defense and voted for him. He always appealed to the common people and did a great deal during the war to see that Georgia troops got needed supplies and that injured soldiers, soldiers' widows, and soldiers' families were supported by the state if necessary.

Perhaps the greatest criticism of Brown as a war governor

was that he saw everything from the Georgia viewpoint, regardless of the needs of the Confederacy. While he attacked President Davis on almost everything, there were some policies of the Confederacy upon which his attacks centered. One of the most fruitful and protracted arguments between Brown and the Davis administration concerned Georgians in the Confederate army. From the time the first Georgia troops were raised for the Confederacy, Brown differed with Davis and the army about the appointment of officers and which troops should be turned over to the Confederacy and which retained by the state. When a conscription law was passed by the Confederate Congress in 1862, Brown disbanded his state troops; but he soon adopted the policy of raising militia from men not subject to Confederate draft. The relentless need of the Confederacy for troops took Brown's state troops almost as soon as they were organized, by increasing the age limits subject to conscription. Brown fought conscription continually, exempted numerous state officials and militia officers, and refused any help to Confederate officers attempting to enforce the law. In several counties in North Georgia where conscription was very unpopular and could never be carried out successfully, Brown's attitude hurt enforcement. Despite the arguments between Brown and the Davis administration over troops, Georgia contributed 120,000 men to the Confederate armies. Brown engaged in an argument at the beginning of the war concerning the ownership and use of state weapons and munitions. He refused to allow Georgia troops to carry state arms out of the state and sometimes refused to allow troops operating in Georgia to use state munitions which were available.

Other Confederate policies which Brown opposed and encouraged Georgians to evade were the impressment of supplies by the Confederate army and the tax-in-kind levied on farm products. The main arguments of the opponents against these policies were that they were illegal, were administered unfairly, and that prices paid for impressed articles were too low. Brown and Davis also differed over the space demanded by the Confederate government on blockade runners operated by the state, and about the seizure of the state-owned Western and Atlantic Railroad by the Confederate army. Finally, there was the argument over the suspension of the writ of *habeas corpus*. Here the contention was that the law allowing suspension was unconstitutional and that there was no real need for the suspensions that took place. Brown encouraged the agitation for peace toward the end of the war, while the Davis administration was demanding that the war be continued.

In most of his opposition to the Confederacy, Brown was ably seconded by Vice President Alexander H. Stephens, the leader of the anti-administration forces in the Confederacy, and his brother Linton Stephens, by Robert Toombs, and to some extent by Herschel V. Johnson. Howell Cobb and Benjamin H. Hill were the leaders of the Confederate forces in Georgia, but since they were often out of the state—Cobb with the army and Hill in the Senate in Richmond—they were not able to oppose Brown as effectively as they might have done in Georgia. Brown and the Stephens brothers undoubtedly held extreme states-rights views and were sincerely worried for fear the Confederate government would create a centralized despotism. But they failed to realize that no government could continue to exist that did not have sufficient power and backing to preserve itself. Often Brown was opposed by the Georgia Assembly, and usually by the majority of the state press. The general consensus in the 1860's and since is that Brown and his group hurt the cause of the Confederacy by their continual opposition to many important policies.

One problem created by all wars is how they shall be financed. While Georgia did not have the primary duty of doing this, the war did bring considerable extra expenses to the state government. Georgia, like the other Confederate states and the Confederacy itself, began the war by borrowing money rather than by increasing taxes. By the end of 1861 Governor Brown had convinced the legislature that, instead of selling bonds, the state should issue treasury notes which could circulate as currency and would not bear interest. By 1862 it was obvious that state taxes must be increased. First, existing taxes were extended in scope and increased in amount, but in 1863 new forms of taxation had to be found. In that year a profit and income tax on articles manufactured and sold in Georgia was enacted. This tax, a graduated one that began at one-half of one per cent, was aimed primarily at speculation and excessive profits. It was poorly administered and often evaded.

The main state war expenses were concerned with supplying troops from Georgia with clothing, hospital supplies, and morale-building comforts; with encouragement of the manufacture of needed items; with purchase of salt and other scarce foods; with removal of indigent non-combatants from combat areas; and with the care of indigent soldiers and their families. The last-named activity was the greatest extra war expense. The income from the profit and income tax was distributed to the counties for this purpose, and state appropriations increased from $2,500,000 in 1861 to $6,000,000 in 1865. They totaled $22,000,000 for the period of the war.

The state's financial and economic life remained in sound condition for the first two years of the war. Inflation came in the last two years despite laws and public sentiment against it. Specie virtually disappeared from circulation, and the paper money—issued by the Confederacy, by the state, and by banks and private companies—that replaced it depreciated greatly in value. Prices increased rapidly, and many commodities rose entirely out of the reach of people with ordinary incomes, such as farmers or soldiers. Sherman's invasion and its great property destruction entirely disrupted much economic life, and the economic chaos that came at the end of the war was a result of military defeat and destruction rather than public or private incompetence.

MILITARY ACTION, 1861–1863

When the war began, the first military concern of Georgians was to defend their coast, which could be attacked easily by the United States Navy. By the winter of 1861, this navy was operating along the South Carolina and Georgia coast. The Savannah River was defended by a small and entirely inadequate fleet of tugs and river boats commanded by Commodore Josiah Tattnall. Confederate and state troops were unable to prevent the occupation of Tybee Island, at the mouth of the Savannah, in November, and other islands throughout the winter. The principal defense effort was directed toward the protection of the city of Savannah and keeping the port open. Land defenses were built, obstructions were placed in the river, and the Confederate commander of the coastal defenses, Robert E. Lee, worked throughout the winter to protect the river from the Federals. Fort Pulaski, the key to the river defense, had been taken over by the state before Georgia seceded. In early 1862, the Federals by-passed Fort Pulaski and cut off its communications with Savannah. After a siege and bombardment, the Fort surrendered to the Federals in April, 1862, and Savannah was effectively closed as a port.

The capture of Fort Pulaski caused renewed efforts to save the city of Savannah itself, but no effort was made to capture it. Control of the river made the occupation of the city unnecessary. Forces were set to work to obstruct all of Georgia's rivers and to keep Federals from using them to invade the state. Throughout 1862 and 1863 coastal raids by Union troops continued, and skirmishes occurred between Federal and Confederate gunboats. In 1862, the Union troops established colonies of slaves from abandoned plantations on the Georgia sea islands and in July, 1863, burned the town of Darien.

In addition to the military and naval activity on the coast, there were two attempts in North Georgia to damage the Western and Atlantic Railroad and thus disrupt the passage of supplies to Confederate armies in Virginia. The first, and more famous, of these raids was carried out by James J. Andrews and some twenty Federal soldiers disguised as civilians who seized the locomotive "General" near Marietta in April, 1862, and managed to get as far as Ringgold before they were captured. The raiders, being pursued by railway personnel, were not able to do much damage. In the spring of 1863, mounted Federal troops under Colonel Abel D. Streight attempted to cut the railroad south of Dalton. Hastily organized local defense units and Confederate cavalry under General Nathan Bedford Forrest prevented damage to the railroad and captured Streight's force though considerably outnumbered by it.

ECONOMIC ACTIVITY

Whether fighting was going on in Georgia or not, manufacturing needed to be increased because of the needs of the war and the cessation of trade with the North and Europe. The war acted as a real stimulus to Georgia industry until Sherman's invasion caused so much physical destruction. The greatest war industry in the state was the manufacture of munitions and army supplies by private individuals, the state government, and the Confederate government. The state followed the policy of making appropriations to encourage new and needed manufactures. The greatest centers of defense manufacturing were Atlanta, Columbus, Augusta, Savannah, and Macon. In all these cities Confederate arsenals were established, and state arsenals in several. Atlanta became a depot center of the Confederate army as well as the location of many factories working on army contracts. Small arms and artillery, powder, ammunition, and pikes and swords were produced. Augusta's Confederate powder works was said to be the largest in the world. Gunboats and engines were made in Columbus, and armor plate and rails in Atlanta.

The manufacture of quartermaster supplies, especially clothing and textiles, was done largely in the fall line cities of Augusta and Columbus. The greatest handicap in textile manufacture was the inability to secure new machinery to replace that worn out or to expand production. In the last two years of the war the Confederacy often established its own factories for the manufacture of quartermaster supplies or contracted for the entire output of existing mills. This increased civilian shortages and encouraged home manufacture in many areas. To help home production of textiles, a factory for the manufacture of cotton cards was established at the penitentiary in 1863, but shortages of wire limited the number of cards which were produced.

There were shortages of skilled labor as well as of materials and machinery. Manpower became so critical that there was a constant quarrel between the Confederate army and state officials about the exemption of skilled workers from the draft. This furnished fuel for the argument between Governor Brown and the army. The one exception to a worker shortage was in the textile field, where many of the workers were women and children. Attempts to found new factories were largely unsuccessful because of a shortage of capital, machinery, raw materials, and skilled labor. However, many small mills or shops were set up to produce items for the local market.

Georgia railroads experienced most of the same problems that her manufacturing establishments encountered. Attempts were made to extend railroads into certain areas lacking them, but no track was actually laid. Throughout the war greater demands were made upon the railroads to transport soldiers and army supplies than they were equipped to handle. The state had few facilities for manufacturing rails and rolling stock, and these suffered from material and labor shortages. It was impossible after 1863 to replace or adequately repair worn out or damaged equipment. There was also the problem of manpower to keep the trains rolling. Skilled railway workers were exempt from army duty, but unskilled were not. Governor Brown carried on numerous arguments with the military authorities about employees of the state railroad who were drafted. When the Confederacy sought to seize the state road and its rolling stock, Brown was able to prevent the seizure.

The final chapter of Georgia's railroads in the Civil War was written by the Sherman campaign of 1864. Much rolling stock and large segments of the Western and Atlantic (between Chattanooga and Atlanta), the Macon and Western (between Atlanta and Macon), the Atlanta and West Point (south of Atlanta), the Georgia (between Atlanta and the Oconee River), and the Central of Georgia (between Gordon and Savannah) were destroyed or badly damaged. Some repairs were made upon these roads before the end of the war; but the Western and Atlantic, which was repaired and used by the United States Army, was the only important road in usable condition when the war ended.

Because so many more Georgians were concerned with agriculture than with manufacturing or transportation, the effect of the war on agriculture was of more immediate concern than anything else except the actual fighting. The war opened with agricultural prosperity and with cotton selling at a higher price than it had brought in several years. As soon as the Federal blockade was instituted, the policy of urging the raising of less cotton and more food crops was begun. Georgia's cotton crop fell from around 700,000 bales in 1860 to 60,000 in 1862; and considerably more provisions were raised in line with the Confederate and state recommendations. Governor Brown recommended a tax on cotton in excess of home needs, but the legislature passed instead a law allowing the planting of no more than three acres of cotton for every farm laborer. Brown recommended additional cotton reduction, but the legislature took no further action. However, the cotton crop for the remaining war years was less than that of 1862. Georgians did a great deal more diversified farming during the war because of a personal need for food, from a desire to supply the army, and because the sale of cotton was difficult as long as the blockade lasted. Corn, small grains, and livestock were probably the items most increased in production. Sugar, fruit, and vegetables were also produced, mainly for local consumption. Until Sherman's invasion, Georgia was one of the important sources of food for the Confederate armies in Virginia.

There was no agricultural labor problem except on farms where there were no slaves. Of more importance to agricultural production was the shortage of competent supervision for the slaves, with many plantation owners and their sons away in the army. Overseers were sometimes available, but many of them went into the army and those left usually needed more supervision than women or old men could give them. When adequate white male supervision was lacking, there was continual fear of insurrection, and increased insolence and failure to work on the part of slaves. In spite of the absence of customary supervision, most slaves continued to do their work and gave no trouble. Individual crimes perhaps increased; but real insurrection, so often feared, did not develop. Many slaves left their plantations when the Federal armies were nearby, but tended to drift back once the army had left, except for the few who accompanied the soldiers.

Slaves were used for army duty, as well as for farm labor. By 1862, slaves were being impressed for work on the Savannah fortifications; and such impressments continued throughout the war, despite the objections of many. As the war progressed, Negroes were used in more and more non-combat army duties. They became teamsters, cooks, nurses, and laborers of all sorts. Toward the end of the war, they were impressed by the Confederate army and used to repair the railroads. In 1863 there was a movement to use slaves for combat duty; most Georgians opposed this, and nothing was done until 1865, just before the end of the war. By this time, many Negroes had left with the armies, flocked to the towns, or were otherwise unavailable for farm work.

SOCIAL AND INTELLECTUAL CONDITIONS

Throughout the war the great majority of Georgians were loyal to the Confederacy. There were two main groups who held Union sympathies, Northerners who had recently come South and natives who opposed secession and slavery. The first group was small and unimportant, though in the thinking of many people early in the war it was a source of considerable danger. Probably, most Northerners who remained in Georgia were loyal Confederates or sought to be neutral—a difficult thing during the war. In mountainous North Georgia, however, there was strong Union sentiment among the people who opposed both slavery and the social and economic system of the lowlands. Many of these persons refused to volunteer or to be drafted into the army. Governor Brown, who was originally from this section and knew the people well, sought early in the war to combat this feeling by giving soldiers and officers from the northern counties favorable treatment. He had some success, and soldiers were raised in all the northern counties, but not in the full contingent according to their population. After Brown began opposing the drafting of soldiers, there was increased trouble in enforcing the draft in the mountainous counties.

Besides draft dodgers and opponents of the war, army deserters often caused considerable trouble. Deserters came from all parts of the state, but tended to come in larger numbers from the mountainous section and the pine barrens, the sections with the lowest social and economic status. Men deserted, as they always have, because they did not like conditions in the army, because they thought it unfair that some were excused from army duty, because they could earn more money outside the army than in it, and because of bad conditions at home. There were deserters who banded together for self-protection and who terrorized sections of the state, especially where there was little local law enforcement machinery or where there was much vacant land where the bands could hide out from the authorities. Frequently, it was necessary to send troops into some areas to arrest bands of deserters or to protect the people there. Desertions were especially bad in Georgia in 1864 because of the havoc that Sherman caused in the state, the war weariness, and the belief of increasing numbers of people that the Confederacy could not hope to win the war. In late 1864 and 1865 it was impossible to enroll conscripts in many counties. In 1865 perhaps as many as one-half of the Georgians subject to military duty were absent from the army.

Despite military action, trouble with the draft and with deserters, farming and manufacturing problems and shortages, and arguments between Governor Brown and the Davis administration, in many ways life in Georgia went on much as it had previously. The people must be informed and entertained, children must be educated, and moral and social problems must be considered by the churches and other organizations.

The most important source of information about local and world happenings continued to be the newspapers. In 1860, there were seventy-two newspapers in the state, twelve of them dailies, with a total circulation of 145,972. Once secession had come, the entire press backed the Confederacy and the war effort. Several important papers were anti-Davis, but more of them supported Davis than Governor Brown in the numerous arguments between the two. The greatest trouble of the newspapers throughout the war was a shortage of paper. Editors and printers were draft exempt, but many of them went to the army anyway. Securing authentic news rapidly was also difficult. The papers followed voluntarily the Confederacy's injunction not to publish military news of value to the enemy, and there were no attempts at censorship. Because of the rising expenses, the scarcity of paper, and editors and printers going to the army, by the end of the war some fifty-three newspapers that existed in 1860 had ceased publication. Some new ones had, of course, been founded; but many of these lived only a

short time. With Sherman's invasion, there was considerable
movement of newspapers to keep ahead of the Federal army,
and every newspaper was forced to suspend publication at
some time during the war.

There were some thirty-three periodicals—literary, religious, agricultural, and miscellaneous—published in Georgia
in 1860. This number grew because the war ended the circulation of Northern periodicals. Perhaps Georgia's leading
periodical was the *Southern Field and Fireside,* published in Augusta, which divided its space into three departments: literary,
agricultural, and horticultural. The *Southern Cultivator,* a
leading agricultural periodical, had a wide circulation
throughout the Confederacy, and was the only newspaper or
periodical in the state that did not have to suspend publication
at some time during the war. By far the most interesting
periodical was the *Countryman,* published by Joseph Addison
Turner at his plantation Turnwold in Putnam County. It was
modeled after the eighteenth century English periodicals and
was filled with "choice miscellany." The author's independence
of mind made this an interesting sheet, but the fact that Joel
Chandler Harris received his literary apprenticeship from
Turner while learning the "printing trade" at Turnwold makes
it even more interesting. Charles H. Smith's humorous stories
signed "Bill Arp," first published in newspapers and later collected into book form, were perhaps the outstanding literary
items produced in the war years.

As is usually the case in wartime, higher education suffered
during the Civil War. Army enlistments took many students in
1861 and almost the entire male enrollment in 1862. The University of Georgia had but two graduating seniors in 1862 and
closed in the fall of 1863 for the duration of the war. Emory
College at Oxford closed in November, 1861. At Oglethorpe
University a class was graduated in 1862 and a few students
attended during 1863–64. Mercer University at Penfield was
the only men's college that remained open, despite small enrollments, throughout the entire war. Enrollment in women's
colleges was not affected by the war. In fact, Wesleyan College
increased its enrollment and only suspended classes temporarily twice when the military situation seemed to demand it.

Several women's colleges were burned during the war and others were taken over by the Confederacy to be used as military hospitals, a use to which the plants of closed men's colleges were often put. Women's schools that were open had a hard time securing competent faculties, the necessary food and clothing for their students, and often had difficulties in obtaining students who could afford the tuition after inflation set in. Medical schools were also casualties of the war. They were closed by 1863 and their plants were used as hospitals, despite the need of more physicians in the Confederacy.

Secondary and primary schools had no problem with a shortage of students (though some students had difficulty in paying the tuition). The greatest shortages were competent teachers, food, and textbooks. Movement of people caused by the war and the need for the labor of students made school attendance irregular. Parents who had the knowledge or inclination often taught their children at home, especially between sessions. While higher education was hurt considerably by the war, primary and secondary schools were not so much affected until Sherman's invasion in 1864.

For its first two years, the war had little adverse effect upon churches and interest in religion. Many prominent clergymen had opposed secession, but all went along with the state and backed the war effort and the Confederacy. All Georgia denominations favored the formation of a new Confederate church organization, and all but the Catholic Church formed such an organization. Georgia's two bishops, Episcopalian Stephen Elliott and Methodist George Foster Pierce, were leaders in their churches and in the religious life of the state, and were generally well received by people of other denominations.

One of the first and most persistent war duties of the churches was work among the soldiers. Supplies were collected, wayside stations maintained, chaplains sent to regiments and hospitals, and much was done for the spiritual welfare of the soldiers. A number of Methodist and Baptist clergymen entered the army as soldiers or officers in the early days, but generally those who went into military service were chaplains, nurses, and agents of benevolent organizations. Most church mission work during the war was done among soldiers except a little among the Cherokee Indians and an increased amount among Negro slaves.

Soldiers were interested in religion, and revivals or prayer meetings were often held in camp during slack seasons of fighting. Bibles, prayer books, and religious tracts were distributed to soldiers; but procurement of these items was difficult. An interdenominational undertaking of Georgia churches was the Soldiers' Tract Association, which published religious tracts in Macon for distribution to soldiers. Both the Methodists and Baptists published special papers for soldier distribution. On the home front the church had a place in raising civilian morale and congregations were often urged to back the war effort. There were numerous fast and prayer days for the Confederacy and collections of all sorts of contributions for soldier comforts.

Departure of clergymen for the army and the lack of new ones (ministerial students were not exempted from the draft) disrupted religious services in some places; military action did so even more. Some churches were destroyed, and many were used for military hospitals in combat areas. Some churches were closed by the Federal troops, especially if the clergyman refused to pray for the President of the United States. Complications of war-time travel made it difficult to hold state and national conferences, conventions, synods, and similar gatherings. But despite all the troubles of the churches during the war, they held their own so far as numbers and membership were concerned, or even made slight increases. Certainly they played an important part in the civilian and military life of the state.

SHERMAN'S CAMPAIGN
AND THE END OF THE WAR

Though the war affected life in Georgia from the beginning, most of the state escaped military action until 1864. Prior to this there had been the coastal action, the cavalry raids in North Georgia, and some combat related to and following the 1863 fighting near Chattanooga. The only sizable area adversely affected by the war was the coast. But Georgia was too important to the Confederacy as a source of supplies and men to escape permanently the attention of the Federal army.

In May, 1864, General William T. Sherman crossed into Georgia from Chattanooga with 99,000 Federal troops and began Georgia's most important military action, the

Chattanooga-Atlanta-Savannah campaign. Sherman was opposed by Confederate General Joseph E. Johnston with some
43,000 men. The Chattanooga-Atlanta campaign followed a
set pattern. Johnston took up well fortified positions which
Sherman flanked, and so compelled Johnston to withdraw to
protect his line of communications with Atlanta. The two armies followed the route of the Western and Atlantic Railroad
all the way, and great sections of its track were destroyed.
Sherman's superior numbers compelled Johnston to abandon
his last defensive position at Kennesaw Mountain in late June
and to withdraw across the Chattahoochee River to defend
Atlanta.

Just as the defense of Atlanta began, Johnston was replaced
by General John B. Hood as commander of the Confederate
army. As Sherman got close to Atlanta, Governor Brown called
out a part of the state militia and put it under the Confederate
commander. Atlanta's mayor called upon every able-bodied
man to report for military duty to help defend the city. Some
Georgians urged that Brown call out all the people to the defense of the state and personally take the field as their leader.
When Davis told Brown that there were no more troops that
could be sent to Atlanta's defense, Brown began a new round
of abuse of Davis and called out every man able to bear arms
between the age of sixteen and seventeen, fifty and fifty-five,
and all Confederate exempts. Negroes were set to work upon
Atlanta's defenses.

After he crossed the Chattahoochee, Sherman sent raiding
parties of cavalry south to disrupt railway communications to
Atlanta, to destroy military supplies, and to try to release the
prisoners at Andersonville. The first two were accomplished.
Hood attacked Sherman's forces at several points around Atlanta but was never able to dislodge or defeat them. During a
forty-five-day siege, the city's rail communications were cut
and it was subjected to continual bombardment. All Hood's
attempts to break the Federal lines were unsuccessful. Having
tried everything that he knew, Hood evacuated Atlanta on
September 1. The Federals immediately moved into the city
and decreed that all civilians must leave. Brown withdrew his
militia from Hood's control to prevent its being drafted into

the Confederate service and taken out of the state. Sherman tried to negotiate with Governor Brown and Vice President Stephens to take Georgia out of the war; but, when he got no response to his overtures, he abandoned them.

After about two months in Atlanta, Sherman ordered its principal buildings, factories, railroad shops, and warehouses destroyed preparatory to evacuation of the city. For several days in mid-November, fire and destruction raged, destroying all the city except about 400 dwellings. Hood went into Tennessee from Atlanta, hoping that Sherman would follow. Sherman sent a part of his army after Hood and with the rest set out for the Georgia coast. In this famous march to the sea there was little organized Confederate opposition; instead, small cavalry detachments or other troops sometimes used harassing tactics against Sherman's flanks or small Federal detachments. Sherman's forces spread over an area from forty to sixty miles wide, entirely cut off from communications or supplies, and "lived off the land" to the fullest. Despite regulations as to what should be taken and how, soldiers took what they wanted or needed. Much that they could not take was destroyed. Food, livestock, and Negroes were often taken. Food, homes, farm buildings of all sorts were destroyed; and for many years "Sherman's sentinels" dotted the Georgia landscape, indicating the route of the march. Tales of Yankee barbarism flourished in the army's wake. The troops lived well, ate well, rode well, and illustrated to Georgians the truth of the statement attributed to Sherman, that "War is hell."

At Milledgeville the Federal troops held a mock session of the legislature (a real one ended just as the troops arrived) and repealed Georgia's ordinance of secession; they burned the penitentiary (all its inmates but four had just enlisted in the Confederate army), warehouses, and factories; but they spared the Capitol, executive mansion, and town. Confederate cavalry under General Joseph Wheeler sent to oppose Sherman succeeded in convincing some Georgians that Confederate troops were no better than Yankee in the matter of taking the supplies that they needed. Sherman's troops arrived at Savannah in December, after destroying approximately one hundred million dollars worth of property in some forty central Georgia counties. All of the coastal area was now in Federal hands and effective opposition to the Yankees throughout the state was at an end. Fighting stopped in May, 1865, and the state government was replaced by Federal military authority after the arrest of Governor Brown and other prominent leaders.

Reconstruction, Bourbonism, and Populism, 1865-1900

RECONSTRUCTION — POLITICAL DEVELOPMENTS

WITH Georgia occupied and controlled by Federal troops and the removal of Governor Brown from office in May, 1865, state government collapsed. Reconstruction was begun in June when United States President Andrew Johnson appointed James Johnson, a unionist who had held no office under the Confederacy, as provisional governor, charged with the duty of restoring Georgia to her proper place in the Union.

In October a constitutional convention was elected with the same voting qualifications as before secession, except that most prominent political and military officials under the Confederacy were disfranchised until they secured presidential pardon. The convention was dominated by conservative unionists, a few of whom had been important in politics before secession. The revised constitution made few fundamental changes in the existing constitution except for inserting the three provisions laid down by President Johnson as necessary to resuming full relations with the United States: voiding the ordinance of secession, abolition of slavery, and repudiation of the debt contracted to help carry on the war. Repeal of the ordinance of secession and abolition of slavery were decisions made on the battlefield, and there could be little opposition to them. Repudiation of the state debt was more difficult, but was carried because President Johnson insisted that it was necessary.

Elections under the new constitution were held in November, and Charles J. Jenkins, a leader of the constitutional convention, was elected governor. The legislature met and ratified the thirteenth amendment on December 9. Governor Jenkins was inaugurated and the provisional state government came to an end. Two United States Senators, Alexander H. Stephens and Herschel V. Johnson, were elected by the assembly; congressmen had been elected by the voters in November. The legislature sought to put Georgia back upon a peacetime basis and to re-establish her relationship with the United States in routine affairs. Most Georgians accepted the military defeat and were now ready to resume their former place in the United States. On the surface, Georgia was reconstructed.

This assembly conferred full civil rights upon Negroes except that Negro testimony against whites was not to be allowed in the courts. There was no consideration of allowing Negroes to vote. The marriage of whites and Negroes was made illegal. Provisions were made for the upkeep of the graves of Confederate soldiers. Veterans were given free tuition at the state colleges and free licenses to peddle anything except "ardent spirits." Throughout 1866 the state government functioned normally, but Federal troops were still in the state.

Before the ex-Confederate states could be fully reconstructed, their representatives must be seated in Congress. The Congress that assembled on December 4, 1865, was dominated by Radical Republicans who were not in agreement with President Johnson on the treatment that the Southern states should receive. This Congress created a joint committee on reconstruction to study conditions in the South and to decide if the Southern states were entitled to representation in Congress. Until this committee reported, no representatives from the ex-Confederate states should be admitted to either house. The main plank in Congressional reconstruction was the fourteenth amendment, submitted to the states in June, 1866, making the Negroes citizens and trying to insure that they would be given the right to vote. Georgia rejected this amendment in November, 1866, as did every other ex-Confederate state except Tennessee.

By March, 1867, the Congressional plan of reconstruction, replacing civil government with military government in every Southern state that had not ratified the fourteenth amendment, went into effect. Georgia was made a part of the Third

Military District, under the command of General John Pope. Many state leaders advised opposition but not open rebellion. Governor Jenkins tried to bring legal action to stay military reconstruction, but the United States Supreme Court refused to take jurisdiction. Ex-Governor Joseph E. Brown, almost alone of Georgia's leaders, advised acceptance of the Congressional plan as the only way to get along with Congress and to secure eventual self-rule again. Brown was considered a turncoat by most Georgians and cordially hated for his advice, which was ignored. Instead, they heaped criticism upon General Pope and his regime. Critical newspapers lost all legal advertising, and the University of Georgia was closed for a short period because a student criticized Pope in a commencement oration. However, Pope retained most of the elected officials of the state and tried to be moderate, a difficult thing at best.

The first duty of the new government was to compile registration lists of all eligible to vote under the fourteenth amendment. This included all Negroes and excluded some 10,000 whites, but the completed registration lists contained a majority of 2000 whites. In the election of delegates to a constitutional convention, many whites refused to vote. Yet only thirty-seven Negroes and nine carpetbaggers were elected. Twelve conservative whites were elected, but the largest group in the convention consisted of 108 native whites who had decided to accept Congressional reconstruction as a necessity. They thus acquired the scornful name, scalawags, from the conservative whites. Most of the leaders were scalawags or Northerners who had come South before the Civil War, and that is undoubtedly the reason that the convention produced a more conservative constitution than was written in other Southern states where carpetbaggers and Negroes dominated. Ex-Governor Brown, though not a member, exercised a modifying influence upon the convention.

This new constitution gave the vote and full civil rights to all male citizens, Negro and white alike. It guaranteed more rights to the common man, black or white. It altered considerably the structure of the lower courts. Married women were given complete control of their own property, which was freed of any obligation for their husbands' debts. The constitution provided for the establishment of a system of general education free to all children of the state and set aside certain funds to support common schools. Atlanta was made the capital in place of the smaller and less interesting Milledgeville.

To pay the expenses of the convention, General Pope called upon the state treasurer for $40,000; but the treasurer refused to pay this without a warrant from the governor. Governor Jenkins refused to approve such a warrant, insisting that there was no legal authority for the expenditure. General Meade, who succeeded General Pope at this juncture, replaced Jenkins, the treasurer, the controller-general, and the secretary of state with military officers. Jenkins hid the great seal of state and deposited $400,000 of state money in a New York bank to keep it out of the hands of the new government.

When the new constitution was submitted to the voters on April 20, 1868, the conservatives tried to defeat its adoption, preferring a continuance of military rule to rule by Negroes, carpetbaggers, and scalawags. Yet the constitution was adopted by an 18,000 majority, and Republican Rufus B. Bullock, a New Yorker who had come to Georgia in 1859, was elected governor over Democrat John B. Gordon by a majority of about 7000. In the legislature, the Republicans had a majority in the senate while the house was almost equally divided between the two parties. Not all white counties voted Democratic nor did all Negro counties vote Republican, and there were accusations of intimidation and fraud by both sides.

The assembly met on July 4, 1868, ratified the fourteenth amendment, and elected as United States Senators Joshua Hill, an old line unionist conservative, and H. V. M. Miller, both of whom were opposed by Governor Bullock. Bullock was inaugurated on July 22, and Georgia was officially reconstructed for a second time.

The election had proved that the conservatives, the anti-Bullock Republicans, and the independents could control the legislature, regardless of the wishes of Bullock and the Radical Republicans. By fall it was clear that Bullock could control neither the legislature nor the voters. In September the legislature, over Bullock's objections, expelled its Negro members;

and in November the Democrats carried the state in the presidential election. In many counties there was a marked decrease in the Republican vote between April and November, apparently the result of Ku Klux Klan pressure against Negro voters. Bullock undoubtedly used his influence to get the legislature to reject the fifteenth amendment in March, 1869, and worked against reseating the expelled Negro legislators. Georgia's members of the United States House of Representatives were seated in 1868 but were excluded after March, 1869, on a technicality. Her senators were not seated.

The joint Congressional committee on reconstruction took evidence on the situation in Georgia in 1868 and 1869. Governor Bullock and his cohort presented ample evidence of the bad conditions in the state but were contradicted by conservatives. Bullock insisted that Klan violence, expulsion of the Negro legislators, and rejection of the fifteenth amendment made the restoration of military rule necessary in Georgia. Return of military rule was Bullock's way of trying to keep the state Republican; he realized that if things were left to the voters, Georgia would go Democratic. On December 22, 1869, when it was plain that the state's vote was necessary to secure the adoption of the fifteenth amendment, Congress returned military government to Georgia under the Reconstruction Act of 1867 and specified that she must ratify the fifteenth amendment to secure readmission to the Union.

General Alfred H. Terry was placed in command, but he retained Bullock as provisional governor. Soon the 1868 legislature was called to meet, with the expelled Negroes reseated but with a number of conservative whites purged by the military. This assembly was one that would satisfy any Radical, but it caused conservatives to expect the worst. It promptly ratified the fifteenth amendment, and, to make a good job of it, ratified the fourteenth again. Senators were elected, with Radical Foster Blodgett leading the list. Expenses of the state government increased remarkably during the period of this legislature, three items in the budget increasing from $26,000 in 1866 to $231,300 in 1870.

Besides these increases, many of which found their way into the pockets of the Radical officials and their friends, bonds were sold too cheaply and the proceeds misapplied, and bonds were endorsed for railroads that had insufficient assets to warrant endorsement under state law; $30,000,000 worth of bond endorsements were authorized, but only $5,733,000 were actually endorsed. In the operation of the Western and Atlantic, the state railroad, the Bullock regime piled up a deficit of $750,000 in two years. In 1870 the legislature specified that the road be leased at not less than $25,000 a month. A company headed by ex-Governor Brown and containing many important Radical politicians and business leaders and such well-known conservatives as Alexander H. Stephens (who later withdrew) was formed and was awarded the lease at $25,000 a month, despite the fact that another company bid $35,000 a month. By this time Brown had been working for several years with the Radicals, arguing that it was impossible to rid the state of them and that it would be better to work with them than to fight them. Benjamin H. Hill at first attacked Brown for this attitude, but in 1869 joined the Radicals for the rest of their stay in Georgia.

The Bullock regime and its Radical legislature satisfied Congress so well that in July, 1870, Georgia was readmitted to representation in Congress. The Senate refused to seat the senators elected by the Bullock legislature in January, 1869, but instead seated Joshua Hill and H. V. M. Miller, the conservatives elected in 1868. Georgia had now been reconstructed for a third and last time, and the power of the Radicals was fast waning. Although the expenses of the state government had increased considerably and there had been other plunderings of the public treasury, she had not fared nearly so badly as had other states, notably South Carolina and Mississippi. Perhaps the main reason for this was the relatively smaller number of carpetbag and Negro legislators in Georgia. Even after Terry's Purge, her legislature still had a majority of native whites who had a stake in Georgia's future, who were relatively honest, and who had no great love for the Negro.

RECONSTRUCTION — ECONOMIC AND
SOCIAL CONDITIONS

Before continuing with political affairs, it will be well to look at the social and economic developments which followed the Civil War and the freeing of the slaves. The first and most obvious change was the new status of the Negro and all that it implied. The most logical thing for any freed slave to do was to test his freedom by leaving the plantation where he had been a slave. Since slavery had meant work, then freedom should mean no work. Consequently, in the summer and fall of 1865, highways and towns were filled with idle Negroes; and if stealing was necessary to eat, then stealing occurred. But had not the war been fought to help the Negro, and would he not get forty acres and a mule at Christmas? A little advance payment could hardly be complained of. When all the things that ex-slaves did in 1865 are considered, it is still remarkable that they did so little that whites considered evil.

Plantation owners tried to get Negroes to work for them, but had little success in 1865 except in areas where the army commanders were willing to give considerable help. In 1866, the situation improved because the hoped-for distribution of forty acres and a mule had not taken place and because of the determined effort of General David Tillson, state head of the Freedmen's Bureau, to make all able-bodied Negroes work. In Middle Georgia the Bureau did an especially good job in getting Negroes to go to work with Bureau-approved contracts. But contracts were new to Negroes, and many refused to stay on a plantation until the crop was harvested. There were also whites who did not fulfill their part of the contracts. There were Negroes, often old and infirm but sometimes able-bodied, who remained on their old plantations when it became certain to them that they must work. Usually Negroes worked better and produced more in 1866 when they worked under some white supervision than the ones (especially on the coast) who worked entirely independent of supervision. Immediately after the war, the best crops were produced in southwest Georgia, a region which the war had not touched physically, and in the northern part of the state on small farms worked by the owners and their families.

The disruption of the farm labor force and the bankruptcy of planters and farmers were responsible for the greatest changes in agriculture which had taken place by 1868. Others followed more slowly as farming and life in general became more stable and crop production increased. Payment of Negro laborers was difficult because of the scarcity of ready money and because many Negroes left to enjoy their wages before the crops were harvested. Several systems of control and payment of agricultural labor were tried before the share-crop system came into general use.

Costs of production, especially for labor and increased amounts of commercial fertilizer, were higher than before 1861. The fear that the acquisition of political rights by the Negroes would result in less work did not materialize; but the supply of labor did diminish as Negroes went west where wages were higher, removed to the towns, or were drawn into railway construction. The amount of land cultivated decreased because planters tended to concentrate on their better lands. Generally scientific farming and productivity per acre and per laborer decreased as the old supervisory system broke down.

In 1870 agriculture had recovered sufficiently to produce the largest cotton crop ever raised—726,406 bales. The greatest recovery came in central and northern Georgia, where there were proportionately fewer Negroes and more owner-worked farms. The coastal plantations never recovered their former wealth or production of sea-island cotton and rice.

Of considerable importance to agriculture and all business was the state's transportation system, of which the railroads were the backbone. In 1865, no railway was in operating condition throughout its entire length except the Western and Atlantic, which had been repaired by the Federal army for its own use. Financially every road was bankrupt. The Georgia and the Central of Georgia railroads began repairs as soon as the war ended and were soon in operation and paying dividends again. They both acquired connecting lines and created larger and better systems. To further its business, the Central of Georgia acquired a steamship line between Savannah and New York. As soon as the financial chaos disappeared, new railway construction began, aided by state endorsement of bonds. Between 1865 and 1873, 840 miles of railroad were constructed in the state, the most important being in the southwestern and northeastern parts where connections were made with out-of-state lines, giving several areas their first rail facilities.

The state government, like most businesses, was in a bankrupt condition when the war ended. Taxes had been cancelled in 1864 and 1865 and the treasury was empty. The state debt of $20,000,000 was reduced to $2,000,000 when the Federal government required that all debts which originated to aid the war be repudiated. During Reconstruction the state's expenses increased and the endorsement of railway bonds added to its bonded indebtedness, but most of these bonds were repudiated after Reconstruction ended.

Most fluid business capital was wiped out by the collapse of the Confederacy. Confederate currency and bonds were worthless, and little United States currency was available at first. In 1872, state banking capital amounted to only $2,000,000. The banks in the best condition were those connected with railroads, especially the Georgia Railroad and Banking Company and the Central of Georgia Railroad and Banking Company. New banks were founded immediately after the war, including national banks in Atlanta and Augusta. It was several years before acceptable security was available upon which loans could be made, and the greatly decreased value of land made borrowing more difficult than it had been previously.

Once the confusion of the ending of the war had passed, many people were sure that a new day was dawning and they hoped to profit from it. In 1865 and 1866 business expanded considerably and new financial, manufacturing, and public utility companies were founded. Perhaps there was more activity and more hope in Atlanta, but there was some in all parts of the state. Gold was mined again in the mountains, and a telegraph line to the West Indies was projected from the coast. It soon became evident that the war had not swept away all wealth. Over 1200 people were excepted from President Johnson's general amnesty because they possessed wealth of over $20,000. Northerners came South hoping to profit from the need for capital and growing business. Many hoped to raise fifty-cent cotton, but few succeeded. Those who settled in cities and engaged in banking, railroading, and other businesses were more successful. Attempts were made to get Northern or immigrant farm and factory laborers to settle in Georgia, but few came.

Economic recovery helped to renew interest in public education. In 1866, a state superintendent of education was appointed to get schools in operation in the counties, and tuition was made free to all white children and Confederate veterans under thirty years of age. This law never went into effect because of the coming of Congressional Reconstruction. The constitution of 1868 specified that education should be at public expense. In 1869 the legislature passed a law providing for public schools, but little was actually done toward founding schools until after the Democrats gained control of the state in 1871.

The University of Georgia reopened in 1866 after being closed for several years, gave free tuition to young veterans, offered new courses, adopted the elective system, and was soon larger and more useful to the state than ever before. In 1871, a branch of the University, the North Georgia Agricultural College, was founded at Dahlonega with part of Georgia's funds derived from the Morrill Land Grant Act of 1862. The next year more Morrill Act money was used to set up an agricultural and mechanical school as an integral part of the University in Athens. The leading denominational schools reopened by 1866, and Mercer and Emory began to grow bigger and stronger. Mercer moved from Penfield to Macon in 1871 and added a law school two years later. Oglethorpe reopened, but it never regained its earlier position and soon went out of existence.

Immediately after the war, the state did nothing for Negro education, but Northern "missionary societies" and the Freedmen's Bureau were instrumental in founding a number of schools where the freedmen could acquire the rudiments of an education, which many hoped would insure success in their changed status. In 1867, Atlanta University was founded through the efforts and contributions of Northern friends of the Negro, and it soon became a leader in higher education for the race. Other colleges, academies, and elementary schools were founded over the state. The Reconstruction government was interested in Negro education, but did little to translate this interest into schools where instruction was given.

The news and editorial columns of newspapers were still the most sought-after reading matter of most Georgians. By 1870, there were more newspapers in the state than there had been in 1860, with most of the gain coming in the last half of the decade, after the high newspaper mortality during the war. Most of the papers were Democratic, and politics took up a great deal of the news and much more editorial space. A few newspapers caught the spirit of the new day and began to urge increased industry and a more diversified agriculture. Charles H. Smith continued to write his homely wisdom under the name of Bill Arp. He performed a real service in making Georgians laugh at conditions about which many of them could do nothing. As for more serious literature, Richard Malcolm Johnston and Paul Hamilton Hayne produced good prose and poetry of which Georgians could be proud. Charles C. Jones, Jr., wrote a two-volume *History of Georgia*, which was not published until 1883, and other serious historical and semi-popular works. Perhaps his glorification of the Confederacy, especially in his addresses to Veterans' meetings, most endeared him to the Georgians of his day.

If Georgians were unhappy and doubtful about things on this earth, they were more hopeful of and interested in the next world. Religion made gains among both whites and blacks. Separate Negro church organizations grew up for the first time and played an important part in the life of the freedmen. Negro churches were often as much concerned with the affairs of this world as with those of the next. Few Negroes continued to attend white churches now that freedom had come, and Negro preachers often became very influential with their flocks. Both races belonged mainly to the Methodist and Baptist churches, but other ante-bellum denominations continued their existence in the state.

The social and economic changes of the Reconstruction period were less spectacular, even considering the new status of the Negro, than were political changes. Some changes had begun before the Civil War, but others came out of the War and the freeing of the slaves. Many of the changes will be traced more fully in the remainder of this chapter and the next one. But first a return to politics after 1872 is in order.

BOURBONISM — POLITICAL DEVELOPMENTS

After Georgia's third reconstruction and because of the strength that the native whites had shown since 1865, Republican domination was impossible. In December, 1870, a Democratic legislature was elected; but, before it met the next fall, Governor Bullock resigned and left the state, to escape almost certain impeachment. This legislature called a special gubernatorial election for December, 1871, in which James M. Smith was chosen governor. Georgia's government was now entirely in the hands of her native white citizens. Henceforth the Republican Party amounted to little in Georgia and soon was divided between the "lily whites" and the "black and tans," so that it could never take advantage of the splits that developed in the Democratic Party. Most Georgians were, of necessity, Democrats, though many ex-Whigs did not relish the name or association.

Almost as soon as the Democrats got control of the state government there was talk of writing a new constitution to replace the carpetbag document of 1868. Not that this was such a bad constitution—in fact it was a good one—but, because it had been written by Republicans, many Georgians felt that it must be replaced. Some of the political leaders were not anxious for a new constitution, but the demand for one became too insistent to be ignored. Finally, a convention assembled in Atlanta in the summer of 1877 to write a new constitution. The one produced was no radical departure from the one of 1868 regarding Negro voting, voting qualifications, public support of education, and certain other features. Because of the troubles of Reconstruction, the convention trusted no government and wrote a lengthy document containing much statutory material that did not belong in a constitution. It specified in detail expenditures for which taxation could be levied, amount of taxes that could be collected, the salaries of officials, and many other limiting details that soon had to be changed by constitutional amendment. General Robert Toombs, the leader of the convention, was especially anxious to see that taxation and governmental expenditures were limited to the very minimum necessary in 1877, with no consideration for the future. This constitution, amended several hundred times, remained the basic law in Georgia until 1945.

Almost as soon as native white Democrats controlled Georgia again, a split was evident in the Democratic Party. One group looked backward to the ante-bellum South while others looked forward to a new South. Robert Toombs and Alexander H. Stephens, both ex-Whigs, led the first group and seemed mainly concerned with good government at low cost and in wiping out any vestige of Reconstruction. The second group, the New Departure or Bourbon Democrats, which soon came to dominate Georgia's government, was made up of people who were willing to forget Reconstruction, have peace between the sections of the nation, and reunite the nation in order to aid business. The South, they held, had made its mistake in being entirely agricultural before the war, and must learn a lesson from its defeat. They gave up the plantation ideal for that of the shop, the factory, and the railroad. Persons who had become Republicans during Reconstruction, like ex-Governor Joseph E. Brown, or who had advised Georgians to accept Reconstruction as inevitable, like Benjamin H. Hill, were soon leaders of the Bourbon Democrats. They were joined by such typical Confederates as Generals John B. Gordon and Alfred H. Colquitt, who were particularly adept at glorifying the Confederacy when that seemed advisable to win votes and yet who looked forward to bigger and better business in the South. The Bourbons were particularly fortunate in having their ideas spread over the state and nation by Henry W. Grady, the popular editor of the *Atlanta Constitution* and peacemaker between the sections. This group of "forward looking" Georgians impressed upon Northerners the changes that were taking place in the South by visits and speeches in the North and in entertainment of visitors to Atlanta during the International Cotton Exposition in 1881 and the Cotton States and International Exposition in 1895. These men truly believed in the "New South" described by Grady in his famous speech.

Bourbon Democrats were interested in business and the urban areas, but largely ignored the small farmers and their interests. In the northern part of Georgia, where there were too few Negroes to justify the cry of Negro domination in order to secure party regularity, a small farmer movement in opposition to the regular Bourbon party machinery grew up in the 1870's. It was first noticeable with the election of Dr. William H. Felton in 1874 as an Independent Democratic congressman in the "bloody seventh" Congressional district in opposition to the regular Democratic candidate. Felton's opposition to the "Atlanta ring" and his championing of the small farmer made him feared by the regular Bourbon politicians, won him three successive elections to Congress, and made him a leader in the opposition to the Bourbons in the state. Another Independent Democrat, Emory Speer, won a seat in Congress from northeastern Georgia in 1878 and 1880. Two other Congressmen of independent tendencies were also elected in 1878. In 1882, it looked as if the Independents were about to capture the governorship with the aging Alexander H. Stephens. However, the Bourbons realized the magic of Stephens' name and prevailed upon him to be the nominee of the regular Democratic Party. This trick effectively killed Independency in Georgia for the decade of the 1880's although Stephens was favorable to many ideas of the Independents and never made a good Bourbon. The three Bourbon leaders (Brown, Colquitt, and Gordon) occupied the governorship and United States Senate seats for most of the period 1876–1890 and, with the help of Henry Grady, controlled most political affairs after the demise of the Independents.

POPULISM — POLITICAL DEVELOPMENTS

By 1890, the Independents were back in the guise of Alliancemen (members of the Farmers' Alliance), and were destined to accomplish much more than they had done as Independents. Throughout the United States, especially in the South, the post-Reconstruction period was a period of agricultural depression. The National Grange, which first tried to relieve the farmers, appeared in Georgia in 1872, and by 1875 had 18,000

members. Its main work was the sponsorship of cooperative
buying and selling agencies for farmers, and educational work
to spread the idea of the farmers' plight and to convince farmers that the government should alleviate this plight. The
cooperative efforts did not succeed, and the Grange itself soon
declined. The railroad regulation provisions of the Georgia
constitution of 1877 may have resulted from the activities of
the Grange.

Many farmer ills—the share crop, crop lien and merchant
financing, freight rates, and the opinion of farmers that many
of the agrarian ills stemmed from financial control by Wall
Street and the "money trust"—led to the feeling that improvement could come to farmers only through governmental
action at the state or federal level. Some realized that better
agricultural methods and less production would help, but few
farmers could improve their methods alone, and none could
do anything about over-production. Out of this situation grew
the Farmers' Alliance, a general term for many specific organizations, in the late 1880's and the 1890's.

The Alliance began as a farmer cooperative, much like the
Grange, and with the same troubles. In 1889 all Alliance organizations, labor organizations, and other farmer organizations met and in cooperation set up a yardstick for judging
political candidates whom Alliancemen would back. This
yardstick demanded cheaper money in the form of legal ten-
der notes and the free coinage of silver, revision of tax laws,
closer regulation or public ownership of transportation and
communication facilities, prohibition of dealings in futures of
agricultural production—in a word, that the government take
a hand in bringing back and guaranteeing continued agricultural prosperity. To these demands Georgia Alliancemen,
numbering over 100,000, added the institution of the sub-
treasury system of governmental loans and storage of staple
agricultural products, abolition of the convict lease system, the
building of good roads, better public schools, and a revised tax
structure that would get a larger proportion of government
income from property other than land.

By the elections of 1890 the Alliance was so strong that no
state candidate dared oppose it. In fact, it had swallowed the

Democratic Party; or, as some Alliancemen soon discovered, the Democratic Party had swallowed the Alliance. Both candidates for governor, William J. Northen and L. F. Livingston, ran on their farm records. The legislature elected was overwhelmingly Alliance, and Georgia's ten congressmen, one of whom was Thomas E. Watson, were Alliancemen or agreed to support Alliance principles. General John B. Gordon adopted enough of the Alliance program to get himself elected to the United States Senate by the Alliance legislature. In fact, most Bourbons discovered that they had always been friends of the farmer. The "Farmers' Legislature" proceeded to enact an avalanche of legislation, much of which was Alliance. The powers of the state railway commission were increased and extended to include telegraph and express companies. A maximum twelve-hour day was set for railway employees, and Labor Day was declared a legal holiday. Bank inspection and regulation were expanded to afford greater security to depositors, and combinations or pools of insurance companies in restraint of trade were forbidden. To aid the farmer, state inspection of fertilizer was improved. Primary elections were regulated to prevent ballot box stuffing. The sale of intoxicating liquors in the vicinity of rural schools and churches was prohibited. A state normal school was created in Athens to train teachers, and a Negro college was established at Savannah. All these new state services required additional money, and so the tax rate was increased by one and one-half mills.

This legislative action was the high tide of the Alliance movement in Georgia, and everything had been done within the framework of the Democratic Party. Many Alliancemen objected to being Democrats and claimed that much more could be done outside the restraining influences of the older party. Out of this feeling came the formation of the People's or Populist Party, whose state and national leader was Thomas E. Watson. The Populists immediately set out to accomplish more than had been done by the Democrats. From 1892 through 1906 there were Populist candidates in Georgia elections, but the party never elected a governor, congressman, or the majority of a legislature. Many Alliancemen never became Populists, because of the fear of Negro domination should the

Democratic Party lose its hold. If the whites split, the Negroes would hold a balance of power in Georgia politics. While it might seem logical for Negroes to vote Populist or Republican, this was not what happened. Because of their ignorance of the real issues and because many of them were controlled by Democratic bosses or landlords, the greater number apparently voted Democratic. Negro votes were often sold for one dollar each, plus barbecue and liquid refreshment before the election. Sometimes large groups of Negroes were marched to the polls and voted in a body by their white "friends and guardians." Thomas E. Watson pointed out the especially great use of Negroes, some of them imported from South Carolina, to defeat him in the congressional race of 1892.

The Populists continued to demand that their program be enacted into law in its entirety rather than in the watered-down Democratic version. The Democrats had much to say about party regularity, the danger of Negro domination (while they continued to vote Negroes and use other corrupt means to control elections), and passed considerable Populist legislation to prevent that party from becoming too strong. In the presidential election of 1896, Thomas E. Watson was the Populist vice-presidential candidate on a ticket with William J. Bryan, the Democratic nominee and backer of free silver. The Populists were not able to come to any understanding with the Georgia Democratic Party about a split of electors in Georgia, so that the Democrats carried the state without any trouble. In the state elections the Populist gubernatorial candidate polled 85,832 votes against 120,827 for the Democratic candidate, the highest vote the Populists ever polled in Georgia. The rising prosperity of the country and state after the panic of 1893, the taking over of Populist ideas by the Democrats, and the Spanish-American War sounded the death knell of Populism. Watson ran for president on the Populist ticket in 1904, but got fewer than 30,000 votes from the entire nation.

BOURBONISM AND POPULISM — ECONOMIC
AND SOCIAL CONDITIONS

Economically, post-Reconstruction Georgia and the South saw

more changes than they had witnessed since the ending of Georgia's frontier in the 1830's. Farming remained the source of livelihood of the majority of the people, but there were numerous and far-flung changes. By the time the chaos of Reconstruction had cleared away, the old plantation system was a thing of the past. Free Negroes resented working in gangs under close supervision as they had done in slavery times. Few planters had sufficient funds to pay money wages throughout the growing season. No system that would keep the Negro at work until harvest time and satisfy him that he had received his just share of the proceeds of the crop could be worked out. Out of this situation there gradually developed the share-crop system in which each tenant family had its own small farm, did its own work with a minimum of supervision, and divided the crop with the landlord at harvest time. This system accelerated the breakup of plantations into smaller farms operated by owners or tenants. Some Negroes and a large number of whites became land owners for the first time, because lower prices made land ownership easier than it had been since the last lands were secured from the Indians.

Share-cropping, once it became common, dominated much Georgia agriculture until well into the twentieth century and, while it produced cotton, did a great deal to hurt the land and the people of the state. Share-croppers, black and white, were caught in the coils of the system and absolutely subject to their landlords and village merchants, often the same person. Because of the ignorance and lack of bookkeeping on the part of the tenants, it was almost impossible for them to secure economic independence, even in good crop years. The landlords and merchants, although they profited more than did the tenants, often became enmeshed in a vicious credit system that caused them heavy losses.

Besides the change from plantation to small tenant farms, which often resulted in considerably poorer farming methods, the greatest agricultural change was in the attitude of the land owners. Large owners now came to consider their lands primarily a source of income, and not the setting for a way of life. Money could be made from capitalistic farming as Governor Colquitt so well proved with his 1000-bale cotton crops in the

1870's and 1880's. Yet the plantation way of life was largely gone and would not return.

There were two ways that farmers could use the government to improve their situation. The more direct method was to control or influence the government as the Independents and Alliancemen tried to do. The more indirect method was to get help through improved agricultural services and scientific research financed by the government. Georgia established the first state department of agriculture in the nation in 1874 and charged it with fertilizer inspection, analysis of soils by a geologist, and discovery and dissemination of useful information to farmers. With the establishment of an experimental farm at state and federal expense in 1888, the state entered actively into agricultural research. Technical improvement of agriculture was originated and backed by the State Agricultural Society, made up mainly of big planters and politicians. It was often opposed by the small farmers because of their inability to see how they would profit directly from the new discoveries and because of the added tax expense.

Much more typical of the Bourbon economic attitude was the desire of businessmen and politicians to increase the railway mileage, trade, and manufacture of the state. Because the Bourbon political leaders were also big businessmen and believed in the industrial growth, they saw that the government was friendly to business and did nothing to hinder it, even though business got no direct aid such as the Reconstruction government had given in its endorsement of railway bonds. Taxation on business, and intangibles such as stocks and bonds, remained considerably lower than on land, and some important politicians profited from such state policies as the convict lease system and the lease of the state railroad.

Perhaps the city of Atlanta typified the Bourbon belief in industry and growth better than any other part of Georgia. Despite its youth, Atlanta had been an important distribution and manufacturing center before Sherman applied the torch in 1864. It rebuilt rapidly after the fighting stopped, its business increased, and the movement of the capital from Milledgeville made it the personification of the new day in Georgia. By 1880, it had surpassed Savannah in population and had become the

88 GEORGIA HISTORY IN OUTLINE

largest city in the state. "Did ever a city grow so?" asked the *Atlanta Constitution* proudly in announcing the new status of the city. Here it was that the Bourbon leaders lived or conducted their business. Here the financial center of the state grew up and much of the new industry was established. Here two great international expositions were held in 1881 and 1895 to boast to Georgia, the South, and the world of the growth of industry. Here it was that visitors listened to Booker T. Washington urge the members of his race to make themselves indispensable by hard work and not to insist upon abstract rights. Here Henry W. Grady and others impressed upon the nation the spirit of the "New South." The *Atlanta Constitution,* under the editorship of Grady and Evan P. Howell, became one of the most widely read Southern newspapers and carried the gospel of industry, wealth, sectional good feeling, and progress over the state, the South, and the entire nation.

Perhaps the most outstanding field of manufacturing and the one that brought the most wealth into the state was that of cotton textiles, which tended to center in the fall line cities of Augusta and Columbus, with many small mills on any stream that furnished sufficient power to turn the machinery. The two cotton expositions held in Atlanta in 1881 and 1895 helped to stimulate cotton textile manufacturing, and by 1900 Georgia ranked third in the South and sixth in the nation in the number of spindles in operation. Besides the manufacture of cotton textiles, Georgians discovered the value of cotton seed; and the manufacture of cottonseed oil, cattle feed, and fertilizers became important by the end of the century.

Georgians also began a more systematic exploitation of their natural resources. Clays were used in brick and pottery manufacture. Coal and iron were mined in the northern part of the state by ex-Governor Joseph E. Brown with convict labor. Timber and timber products, important in Georgia since its founding, continued to be important, especially the hardwoods of the northern counties and the pines in the southwest after both areas were made more accessible by new railroads. By 1900, improved transportation in the pineland region of South Georgia gave the state first place in the nation for naval stores production.

Georgia manufacturing was in the beginning stage, which meant more profits for the owners—often out-of-state capitalists—and low wages for the workers. One of the big inducements attracting industry to Georgia was the low wage scale prevalent in the state. Another was the practice of ten years' tax exemption allowed to new textile and iron manufacturers until this practice was stopped by the constitution of 1877. Throughout the 1880's, several attempts were made to legislate a ten-hour day for factories and to prevent the employment of children under twelve years of age. Such laws failed to pass, despite numerous petitions of laborers and favorable testimony of some factory owners. During the same decade there were some strikes, especially in the Augusta cotton factories, over wages. The Knights of Labor made an unsuccessful attempt to take advantage of these labor troubles and to organize the textile workers. By 1890, picketing by laborers had been outlawed, an eleven-hour day or sixty-six-hour week in cotton and woolen factories had been prescribed, and various safety precautions, especially in regard to women, had been enacted into law.

In social affairs as well as in economic, the Bourbons and their successors had new and "progressive" attitudes. Plantation mansions and their way of life declined; and planters moved to the towns and cities, which gained a new importance. Crossroads or county-seat merchants took on a new importance in the economic pattern of tenant farming, and the business class gained a new social respectability. Many old families combined trade or manufacturing with planting, while those people who depended entirely on agriculture lost economic and social position. Another changed social and economic attitude was the increasing realization that the individual could not be entirely self-sufficient and that government must be concerned with more things than formerly. This contradicted the old Jeffersonian ideal that the least government is the best government. There was objection to government's undertaking new activities, especially for the newly-freed Negro. There was considerably more objection to having to pay more taxes—most of which still came from land—to support these new functions. Yet governmental activity and taxation increased.

A problem that began with Reconstruction and did not end

until the twentieth century was the convict lease system; it troubled the consciences of many Georgians, but nobody seemed able to suggest a satisfactory substitute that did not cost too much. The destruction of the penitentiary by Sherman and the greatly increased number of convicts, mainly Negro, were responsible for the original leasing of convicts to private individuals by the Reconstruction government. The greatest objections to the practice were that it made no attempt at reform, that it allowed private individuals to make a considerable profit out of the labor of prisoners, and that cruelty inevitably resulted from inadequate state supervision of private lessees. There were numerous legislative and executive investigations, many new laws, new methods to see that the welfare of convicts was safeguarded, fines upon lessees who did not carry out the letter of the law, and much opposition to the practice throughout the entire period, especially by the Alliancemen and Populists during the 1890's.

A problem that affected considerably more people than the convict lease system was that of the consumption of strong drink. This was an old problem, but it took on added weight after the Negro was freed from plantation discipline by emancipation. First, liquor was banned from the immediate vicinity of churches and schools. Next, at the request of individual counties, the legislature prohibited the sale of liquor in these counties. By 1881 there were forty-eight dry counties in the state; and the temperance forces made an effort to get a general local-option law passed that would allow any county to vote itself dry without legislative action. Such a measure was enacted in 1885. At first, it proved a real weapon in the hands of the drys, but when the wets had time to consolidate their forces they regained several counties by 1890. The move for statewide prohibition of the manufacture or consumption of liquor was defeated in the 1890's. One of the main arguments used by the wets was that the tax money derived from the sale or manufacture of liquors went to the school fund.

The constitution of 1877, more concerned with education than liquor, provided that the state could levy taxation for elementary schools and the state university. Educational support throughout the rest of the century was derived from a number of taxes or other funds especially set aside by law and not by appropriations from the state treasury. This income increased from $174,000 in 1871 to over $1,000,000 by 1900, but it was always insufficient for anything like an adequate educational system. The public schools began to take shape when Governor James M. Smith appointed Gustavus J. Orr as State School Commissioner, a position which Orr held from 1872 through 1887 and in which he became the real "father of the common school system in Georgia." Under Orr's leadership, funds were increased and workable systems at state and county level were instituted. In most rural areas, financial support of education came entirely from the state, but wealthier counties and cities often supplemented state support with local taxation. Control of schools was always in the hands of local boards.

By 1900 six months of free schooling was available to children in many counties. Yet many Georgians were still unwilling to carry out Commissioner Orr's suggestion that a state-wide school system be established which would furnish over six months' education to all children, black and white. Publicly supported high schools were yet to come, and many people were sure that Negroes needed little if any education.

With the increased school enrollment and lengthened terms, there was a need for more and better trained teachers. Around 1890, two normal schools were founded (at Milledgeville and Athens), whose special task was to train teachers for the public schools. The Georgia School of Technology was chartered in 1885 and soon began operation in Atlanta as the center for technical training so necessary in an industrial age. Special appropriations were made by the legislature for the founding of new schools and for special needs, but no regular appropriations were made for higher education. Except for student tuition, the only regular income of the University of Georgia throughout this period was the interest paid by the state upon the money derived from the sale of the University's original landed endowment and the lands granted under the Morrill Land Grant Act of 1862.

Higher education for Negroes received its first state appropriation in 1873 when $8000 was voted to Atlanta University, an existing private institution in Atlanta. This appropriation continued until 1888, but in 1890 it was transferred to the Georgia Industrial College, a state school which opened at Savannah in 1891. Negro denominational colleges secured considerably more private funds than did white ones, so that by 1900 the several Negro colleges located in Atlanta and elsewhere throughout the state had more wealth than the white colleges in the state.

Private academies continued to operate throughout the state, sometimes with partial support from local government. The denominational colleges increased in size and usefulness, occasionally aided by gifts from Northern philanthropists. Additional denominational or private colleges were founded toward the end of the century and these considerably augmented the educational facilities of the state, if not the caliber of instruction offered. The prevailing type of curriculum was classical and aimed at training for the professions, although a beginning was made in agricultural and mechanical education, a form which would expand considerably in the twentieth century. An unfortunate practice of the schools, both public and private, was that they attempted to do much more than their financial resources could support adequately. It was impossible to get sufficient funds to create a really adequate public school or university system.

In religious affairs, conditions in Georgia were somewhat better than in the field of education. The confusion caused by the war and Reconstruction was remedied—congregations were reconstituted, pastors were secured, and church buildings were repaired or built. The increased wealth of the cities was largely responsible for the construction of new and pretentious church buildings. The separation of Negro worship from white became complete, and Negro church and Sunday school organizations were created or expanded. The Methodist and Baptist churches continued the leadership in number of members and in all phases of church work.

In the field of social service, the state government was just beginning to function in the last quarter of the nineteenth century. One group of Georgians to whom the state felt that it owed an increasing debt of gratitude was the Confederate veterans. Immediately after the war, the state voted veterans who had lost

a leg or an arm free artificial limbs, and offered free tuition at
the state university to all ex-soldiers who desired it. A commissioner of pensions was set up in 1896, and two years later a state
home for old soldiers was created.

Beyond aid to former Confederates, the state did little toward
caring for its unfortunate citizens except to expand the facilities
provided at the state mental hospital, the academy for the deaf,
and the academy for the blind. It was the Bourbon, and not the
Republican, state government that first admitted Negroes to
these institutions and that did more to promote the expansion of
each of them than did the Reconstruction or Alliance governments. During the Bourbon period there was a general feeling
of increased social responsibility on the part of the state, and
increased appropriations were made despite the opposition to
raising taxes or increasing governmental functions. All other
help to unfortunates was carried on by local governments,
churches, and private agencies.

CHAPTER SIX

Twentieth-Century Georgia

POLITICAL DEVELOPMENTS

⌊Twentieth-century Georgia politics began with the decline and speedy demise of the Populist Party and the adoption of Populist principles by reforming Democrats. Confederate soldiers and Bourbons quickly faded from the political scene along with the conception that politics was reserved for "gentlemen." The "wool hat boys" aroused by the Populists soon took control of Georgia politics and have retained control ever since. During the administration of James L. Terrell (1902–1907) there was almost an "era of good feeling" in Georgia politics, with a united Democratic Party as the only active political organization in the state. But such a condition could not last. In fact, the election of 1906 was as bitter a contest as Georgia had seen in a long time. The chief rivals for the governorship were Clark Howell, editor and publisher of the *Atlanta Constitution,* and Hoke Smith, a former owner of the *Atlanta Journal,* who was supported fully by that newspaper. Thomas E. Watson backed Smith's progressive program and his advocacy of eliminating the Negro from politics. One especially strong plank in Smith's platform was a demand for further railroad regulation. Howell was pictured by his opponents as the friend of the railroads. Two such friends of the common man as Smith and Watson proved irresistible. Smith won the primary by a great majority and had no real opposition from the Populist candidate in the general election.

Georgia, like the other parts of the nation, was ready for a reform administration. The way had been paved already by a state pure food and drug act and by restrictions on child labor in factories. Under Smith the legislature cooperated in a reform program that included increasing the powers of the railroad commission over railroads and giving it control over other public utilities, subjecting other types of business to increased supervision, enacting statewide prohibition, and abolishing the convict lease system. Primary elections were regulated by state law; campaign expenditures must be published, and financial contributions by a business corporation to a political campaign were forbidden. The most important political change during Smith's administration was the elimination of the Negro vote by the use of the "grandfather clause," which was adopted as an amendment to the state constitution in 1908. To vote, one must be a United States or Confederate war veteran or a descendant of one, a person of good character who understood the duties and obligations of citizenship, a person who could read and write a paragraph of the United States or Georgia constitution, or the owner of forty acres of land or property worth $500. Few Negroes could meet any of these qualifications, but most whites could meet at least one of them.

State politics during the next two decades was devoid of new or important ideas and throve mainly on personal animosities during political campaigns. Thomas E. Watson, until his death in 1922, was the most influential political leader in the state, and he often determined elections by indicating which way his personal following of "wool hat boys" should vote. All Georgia politicians stood for the same thing—white supremacy, the Democratic Party, lowered taxes and a minimum of governmental services, and friendship for the common man. National and international affairs, especially during World War I, often outweighed state affairs in interest.

One of the most celebrated political events of the period was the case of Leo Frank, a Jew convicted of assault on a young gentile woman in his employ. Governor John M. Slaton did not believe that the evidence upon which Frank was convicted was conclusive; so he commuted the death sentence to life imprisonment, despite the unpopularity of such action. Race hatred was stirred up by Thomas E. Watson in his newspaper, and Frank was taken from the jail and lynched by an angry mob in September, 1915. The Frank case was not an isolated incident but exemplified a general tenor of feeling, as was illustrated by the refounding of the Ku Klux Klan a few years later and its quick spread over the state, the South, and the nation. The

Klan became a "100% Americanism" organization which followed Thomas E. Watson's program of opposition to Negroes, Jews, Catholics, and foreigners. It became such a force in state politics that most office seekers considered Klan membership a prerequisite to election. In rural Georgia, depression made itself felt as soon as the prosperity of World War I ended. While the state could not increase its bonded indebtedness, it did pile up an operating deficit for several years. Governor L. G. Hardman (1927–1931) tried in vain to get the legislature to revamp the governmental organization and tax structure to meet these deficits. When Richard B. Russell, Jr., became governor in 1931, the depression had reached its depths, and he was able to get the legislature to follow his lead in a thorough governmental reorganization. Administrative offices, boards and commissions, and other agencies which had grown up over half a century were consolidated, eliminated, or revamped until the state had a much more efficient organization and one cheaper to operate. Appropriations were reduced and brought within income, and Georgia was given an up-to-date organization to carry on the increased duties of state government that had come with the twentieth century: Having made such a good showing in Atlanta, Russell was anxious to move on to Washington. This he did in 1933, after the death of Senator William J. Harris.

The decision of Russell to run for the United States Senate brought eight candidates into the gubernatorial race in 1932. The victor, Eugene Talmadge, is perhaps the most typical and certainly the best known and most controversial political figure in Georgia since the day of Tom Watson. "Gene" Talmadge, like Watson, was fully aware of the fact that the Lord had made more common people than any other sort. He also realized that two-unit-vote counties were the ones which determined elections in Georgia and boasted that he was elected "where the street cars don't run." His philosophy of economy in government and reduction of taxes, reduction in governmental services, and insistence with Jefferson that the least government is the best government, appealed to both the common folk and the wealthier classes. An adept showman and psychologist,

Talmadge used three-dollar automobile license tags, red gal-
luses, insistence upon white supremacy, and the aiming of his
campaign oratory at his most uneducated hearers as the political capital that secured his election to the governor's office four
times and created a political tradition which is still powerful in
Georgia.

Once Talmadge was in office, his belief in himself and his
program, regardless of the opposition of other elected officials
or the legislature, soon brought the term dictator to the lips of
his enemies. But there is little evidence that the majority of the
people did not approve his program or the way he carried it
out. When the legislature refused to reduce the cost of automobile license tags to three dollars, a campaign pledge,
Talmadge did it by executive order, and thereby probably endeared himself to more people than by any other act of his
political career. When the legislature adjourned without passing an appropriation bill in 1935, Talmadge continued the last
appropriation bill in force. When the highway commission refused to carry out certain orders of Talmadge or resign, he
declared martial law and used National Guardsmen to oust the
commissioners and to install his nominees. He used the same
tactics when the treasurer and comptroller-general refused to
sanction his expenditures of state funds without an appropriation bill. Talmadge soon came into conflict with federal officials
in Washington. Indeed, he could hardly avoid doing so, since
his entire political philosophy was almost diametrically opposed to that of the Roosevelt New Deal. The first differences
were over federal aid to state highways; later differences concerned the NRA program of minimum wages, the distribution
of or existence of federal relief funds, federal crop control and
benefit payments to farmers, old age pensions, and public
health. It was possible to camouflage the benefits of these programs to Talmadge's rural supporters through appeal to the
idea of Yankee interference with Southern ideals, and especially to the fact that the program gave the same consideration
to Negroes as to whites. Much of the state press, the farmers'
organizations, and certain other groups objected to Talmadge's attitude and backed the New Deal. The worst textile
strike of the state's history, in 1934, was handled by Talmadge

by a declaration of martial law, the use of National Guardsmen, and the arrest of many strikers. In 1936 Talmadge received a double defeat. In his personal race for the United States Senate against Richard B. Russell, whom he characterized as a "rubber stamp of Washington bureaucrats," he was soundly beaten. His handpicked candidate for governor, Charles D. Redwine, was defeated by Eurith D. Rivers, who promised cooperation with the New Deal in Washington. Perhaps Talmadge had misjudged the strength of Roosevelt in Georgia or of his own popularity. However, he was far from dead in Georgia politics.

With the election of Rivers and a friendly legislature, Georgia for the first time could fully enter into the philosophy, services, and payments of the New Deal. The legislature passed, and the people approved by constitutional amendment where necessary, laws granting old age pensions, health services for all, additional relief funds for the disabled, tax exemptions for $2000 value of homestead and $300 for household furniture and tools, classification of property as tangible and intangible for tax purposes and different rates for different types of property, seven months of school for all with free textbooks, and pay increases for teachers. To prevent future dictatorial rule by a governor, the legislature secured the right to convene itself into extra session, if necessary.

In 1938 Rivers' new program was going full blast and he was re-elected without difficulty. It was the senatorial race in 1938 that attracted the interest of most Georgians. Walter F. George, a conservative Democrat who had opposed President Roosevelt's "court-packing" plan, ran for re-election. George was one of the senators picked by Roosevelt to be purged as too conservative to suit the New Deal philosophy, and Georgians were asked to send Lawrence S. Camp to the Senate in his place. Talmadge ran also and very nearly defeated George; Camp ran a poor third. For many Georgians the year 1938 ended the belief that Franklin D. Roosevelt could do no wrong, a belief that had persisted since 1932.

By the opening of his second term, Rivers began to have trouble finding enough money to pay for the added services which his program had instituted. The new intangibles tax did not bring in the anticipated revenue, and the sales or chainstore tax advocated by Rivers failed to pass. Many favored the repeal of prohibition and the use of alcoholic beverages as a new source of taxes, but repeal proved impossible. A local option law passed in 1938 brought in some revenue. The state was forced to scale down appropriations as much as 25% except for a few services like debt reduction and the salaries of school teachers. Rivers tried to levy on the highway funds for other state expenses and met opposition from the state highway board. Like Talmadge, he eventually used martial law to get control of the highway department and, after a fight in the state and federal courts, secured the money he sought. Yet, at the end of his second term, the state deficit had reached $22,000,000, a sizable figure.

In 1940 Rivers had served the two terms allowed to a governor by the Georgia constitution, and the large state deficit made obvious to all the high cost of his new program. Former Governor Talmadge, now eligible to run again, entered the race and was elected. Most of the Rivers program was continued, despite the different philosophy of Talmadge. But the greatest excitement in Talmadge's third term was caused by his determination to discharge certain faculty members of the University of Georgia and other units of the University System because of his belief that they advocated the admission of Negroes to the state's white colleges. The Board of Regents refused to follow up the governor's recommendations or to be convinced of his opinions. He got rid of certain regents whose terms had not yet ended, regardless of his legal right to do so, and appointed new regents who made it possible to dismiss the designated faculty members. Accrediting agencies of colleges, universities, and professional schools removed all the schools in the University System from their accredited lists. Thus national standing of the entire University System was abolished, with the result that degrees of current graduates would be rendered worthless professionally. The entire state was aroused.

Just at this juncture a gubernatorial election came due, and Talmadge found himself opposed by Ellis Gibbs Arnall, a young state attorney general who vowed to remove control of the University System from politics. All over Georgia students and friends of the University opposed Talmadge, as did almost the entire state press. To the surprise of many Georgians, Arnall won the election. Georgians thus conclusively demonstrated that they did not want their schools or University System made a political football and that, if aroused, they would fight for them. True to his campaign promises, Arnall pushed a reorganization of the Board of Regents. The governor was removed and the Board enlarged. With lengthened and staggered terms, it would now be difficult for any governor to appoint a majority of the Board. Georgia's colleges were again included on the accredited lists. Arnall also pushed a general reorganization of the state government and the establishment of a state civil service system.

Two issues that the governor supported and that achieved favorable national recognition were the granting of the vote to eighteen-year olds (Georgia was the first state to do so) and the repealing of the poll tax as a prerequisite for voting.

Arnall also gave his attention to the state prison system, whose county work camps increasingly were being attacked. A board of corrections was created and given general responsibility for overseeing all state prisoners. A new penitentiary was established at Reidsville, but the prison camps were not abolished.

Arnall favored the revision of the constitution of 1877, which by 1943 had been amended over 300 times. A commission of twenty-three members (including the governor, state officials, lawyers, and laymen) was created to write a new constitution. In 1945 the commission presented its recommendations for revision. After approval by the voters, this document became the constitution of 1945—not really a new document but a revision of the old constitution.

Political scientists and many Georgians would have liked more changes—for instance, the elimination of the county unit system or the elimination of much statutory material—but the commission was guided by the practical consideration of what it thought would be accepted by the voters. Salaries of legislators and state officials were generally increased, and power to change salaries was given to the legislature. A lieutenant governor was provided for, certain boards were given constitutional status, and steps

were taken to initiate a merit system in state civil service. All
mention of primary elections was eliminated, in the hope of
getting around United States Supreme Court action to increase
Negro voting; and eighteen-year-old voting was provided for.
The allocation of certain types of income to specified services or
departments was ended, and henceforth all state income had to
be paid into the treasury and all funds appropriated by the
legislature. Action was taken to allow local governments to bor-
row more money and to have more control of local affairs.

Arnall's progressive administration and revised constitution,
however, were no proof that Georgians had changed their ideas
about politics and political leaders. In fact, the next year ex-
Governor Eugene Talmadge was again elected governor on a
white supremacy campaign set off by the outlawing of Georgia's
white primaries by the federal courts. James V. Carmichael,
backed by Arnall, received the largest number of votes ever cast
for a candidate in a gubernatorial primary in Georgia, but the
county-unit system gave the nomination to Talmadge, who was
elected in the general election.

Talmadge, however, did not live to be inaugurated for a
fourth term; Joseph E. Brown, therefore, is the only man to
occupy the governor's office for four terms. Now a controversy
developed over who should be inaugurated as governor. Herman E. Talmadge, the thirty-four-year-old son of Eugene Talmadge, had received 675 write-in votes in the general election
(perhaps because of his father's illness), which gave him the
second highest number of votes for governor. The legislature
declared that Herman Talmadge and not Melvin E. Thompson,
the lieutenant governor elect, should be installed as governor.
Arnall refused to give up the office, siding with Thompson, but
Talmadge forcibly took possession of the executive offices and
the governor's mansion. For sixty-seven days he occupied the
governor's office, until the state supreme court ruled that
Thompson should have been installed as governor.

Talmadge retired from office, but the next year he ran again
at a special election to fill the last half of the original term. His
successful election campaigns in 1948 and 1950 were an echo of
his father's. Negroes were becoming more insistent on their
rights under the Fourteenth Amendment, and the cry of white

supremacy, always a surefire battle cry with white rural voters, plus the magic name of Talmadge, carried young Talmadge into office. In office he showed his abilities as a politician and administrator and his belief that the appeals of his father's day were not enough for his own. He used the cry of white supremacy, but he also pushed through a sales tax, cut state property taxes, increased funds to schools and other service activities of the state—an increasing share of which was going to Negroes. In an attempt to bypass the U.S. Supreme Court rulings on segregation and to discourage Negro applications to white schools, an effort was made to improve Negro schools by enriching curriculum, improving facilities, and raising teachers' salaries. While the state was devoting over half of its income to public education, it approved a state-subsidized private school plan to replace public schools should integration be ordered.

In January, 1955, Talmadge retired from the governorship and politics until 1956, when he decided to run against Senator Walter F. George. George did not run, and Talmadge easily defeated M. E. Thompson in the primary. Marvin Griffin became governor and continued to increase educational expenditure and to insist that no integration would take place in Georgia schools. Corruption in state government was charged by many against the Griffin administration.

In 1959 Griffin was replaced by Ernest Vandiver, who campaigned on an "up-to-date" program which advocated a badly needed reorganization of the state government and opposed school integration. While Vandiver was concerned with both problems after coming into office, integration often pushed reorganization out of the headline post.

As it had in Eugene Talmadge's day, the Talmadge faction continued to appeal primarily to the rural voters in two-unit counties, while the anti-Talmadge forces appealed to the more affluent whites in urban areas and blacks. Into this rather neat package came a bomb—the 1962 federal court decision outlawing Georgia's county-unit system used in primary elections. In the gubernatorial campaign of that year, conducted on a popular vote' basis, young and forward-looking Carl Sanders defeated the more traditional ex-Governor Marvin Griffin. In

1962, as well, Leroy R. Johnson became the first black member of the legislature in the twentieth century.

The courts soon handed down a decision that the state legislature also must be reapportioned in line with population. The senate was reapportioned in 1962 and the house in 1965. Now for the first time in many a day, people and not geography were represented in the Georgia legislature.

So many white Democrats objected to President Lyndon Johnson's support for the 1964 Civil Rights Act that in the 1964 presidential election Senator Barry Goldwater carried Georgia into the Republican column for the first time ever. The party had been growing in the suburban areas, but now there were wholesale additions of segregationists and states' righters. Goldwater's victory helped to elect Georgia's first Republican congressman since Reconstruction, Howard H. Calloway, and a number of state legislators.

In 1966 Calloway ran for governor against Democrats Ellis Arnall and Lester Maddox. Arnall, twenty years out of politics, seemed curiously dated to many people. Maddox, an avowed segregationist, was the self-proclaimed "friend of the People" and was the victor in a runoff primary. There were now two very different types of conservatives opposing each other. As a result of a write-in campaign for Arnall, no candidate received a majority of the votes, and the Democratic legislature selected Maddox as governor.

Such political strife drove voter participation to new heights, but much of the old glamour of Georgia politics seemed a thing of the past as TV appearances replaced courthouse speeches and barbecues. In the 1968 presidential election Georgians gave Independent Party candidate George C. Wallace first place, Republican Richard Nixon second place, and Democrat Hubert H. Humphrey third place. In 1972 Republican Richard Nixon took 75 percent of the Georgia vote.

In state affairs, Maddox as governor had no real program nor organization, and this helped the legislature to secure more power. In 1970 Jimmy Carter was elected governor and Maddox lieutenant governor. Maddox allied with Carter opponents in the legislature to oppose most Carter programs. Carter came into office proclaiming that the time for racial discrimination had passed. He was concerned as governor with environmental matters, historic preservation, and massive governmental reorganization. George Busbee succeeded Carter in 1974 without any obvious changes in political style. Undoubtedly the greatest sign of change in state and national politics was the election of Jimmy Carter as president in 1976, the first Georgian ever to occupy that position in our nation's history.

There are certain political items that have not been included in the foregoing chronological treatment. One of these is primary elections. These developed on a county level in the last quarter of the nineteenth century, but they were not mandatory. The first statewide primary was held in 1898 to nominate a governor and other state officials. Primaries were a part of the movement to give the common man more direct participation in the government, but in the South they also developed into a method of disfranchising the Negro. With the disappearance of the Populist Party and the universal adoption of the primary for state and local elections, about the turn of the century, the primary became the real election and came more and more to be regulated by the legislature instead of by the Democratic Party. The use of the county-unit rule in primaries was first a party rule, but it became state law in 1917.

Because of the increasing complexity of twentieth-century life, it was necessary to make some changes in the judicial branch of the state government. A court of appeals was created in 1906 to relieve the supreme court of part of its cases. In the early years of the century, city courts, sometimes known as county courts, were created in urban counties to relieve the superior courts of less important cases; and municipal courts replaced justices of the peace. In the larger counties juvenile courts were created to give special attention to young offenders and to place more emphasis on rehabilitation. The superior courts remained the backbone of the Georgia judicial system, regardless of other courts that were created.

The constitution of 1877 specified that no new counties should be created, and this rule was followed for a quarter of a century. But between 1904 and 1924 twenty-four new counties were created by constitutional amendment. This was due mainly to political maneuverings, motivated largely by the desire of certain towns to become county seats and thus gain added importance and wealth. Much was said about county consolidation, but the only consolidation that took place was in 1931 when Milton and Campbell counties united with Fulton. This left 159 counties in Georgia, a larger number than any other state except Texas.

The twentieth century opened with common schools the greatest item of state expenditure and the general property tax the largest source of income. Soon highway costs became a major expenditure. Governmental services, costs, and taxes have increased throughout the century much more rapidly than ever before. Education and highways were the leaders in expenditure until about 1970, when public welfare and health replaced highways in second place.

Because of the need for more money, the legislature has constantly sought additional sources of revenue, generally adding new taxes to the old pattern and giving little consideration to an overall tax revision. Railroads and other businesses that largely escaped assessment in the nineteenth century were taxed. Income, automobile registration, and gasoline taxes have furnished the major new sources of revenue. In 1951 a 3 percent sales tax was levied and immediately became the largest single revenue producer of the state. The per capita contribution to the state government rose from $1.43 in 1900 to $516 in 1974. A long-standing campaign has been waged to equalize taxation and assessments throughout the state and to make assessments according to the type of property. Traditionally, real estate has borne more than its just share of the burden, and intangibles have been under assessed. Yet Georgians have generally been lower taxed than most Americans.

During the first three decades of the century, the state had no real budget system that balanced expenditures against income. In 1933 this situation was remedied when a bureau of the budget was created in the executive office; auditing machinery was established, and a provision was made to reduce appropriations to meet income. Throughout the century the state's bonded indebtedness has been decreased $100,000 a year, as the constitution specifies; few new bonds have been issued, and the net effect has been that Georgia has a remarkably small debt.

ECONOMIC AND SOCIAL CONDITIONS

Farming, though of decreasing importance, in 1900 was still the main source of income for most Georgians. The century opened with expanding agricultural production and income. The value of farm property and crops, the amount of land cultivated, the number of farms, and the number of tenants all increased. Cotton, the major crop, reached an all-time high of 2,769,000 bales in 1911. World War I brought high agricultural prices and increased prosperity. With the end of the war, an agricultural depression set in almost at once, greatly aided by the boll weevil, which arrived in force about 1920. Much farm land was abandoned, and agricultural production declined greatly. Many people, black and white, left the farms and congregated in towns and cities, in and out of Georgia.

Crop control, benefit payments, and resettlement work of the New Deal, plus added technical advice to farmers from local, state, and federal governments, made Georgia agriculture healthier by about 1940 than it had been since the early days of the century. World War II brought labor shortages but increased prosperity. In the period since 1940 agriculture has changed more than at any time since the Civil War brought an end to the old plantation system. The trend has been toward greater mechanization, fewer farm families, fewer and larger farms, larger yields per acre, the almost total elimination of tenant farming, decline in cotton production, and the decline of agriculture in economic importance. In the early 1970's poultry produced one-third of farm income, livestock and dairying another third, and row crops the other third. Major row crops are corn, soy beans, peanuts, and tobacco, with cotton at the bottom of the list.

The changes in farm life began in the 1930's but have come all the more rapidly since 1945. Paved roads, easy transportation, increased prosperity, electricity, and radio and television have ended the isolation of farm life and done much to bring farmers into the mainstream of American life. Farming has benefited from improved agricultural research and education. The Georgia State College of Agriculture was established in 1906 in Athens to give instruction and to conduct research. In the same year an agricultural and mechanical school was founded in every congressional district of the state to provide vocational training in farming methods. Two experiment stations, at Griffin and Tifton, were established to do research. Speakers and pamphlets from these institutions helped to transmit knowledge of improved methods. Getting new information to farmers was greatly facilitated by the Extension Service established in the United States Department of Agriculture during the Wilson administration, which brought a new day in federal, state, and local cooperation.

At the time of the reorganization of the University System in 1932, the Extension Service, the College of Agriculture, and the two experiment stations were all united administratively under the University of Georgia. The district agricultural and mechanical schools were abolished. Their work is now carried on in the vocational programs of the local high schools.

Agricultural research has resulted in the elimination of many plant and animal pests and diseases—the cattle tick and hog cholera, in particular. Unfortunately, the most destructive pest, the boll weevil, is yet to be controlled completely. The experiment stations and agricultural schools have helped with the crop diversification, and many new crops have been developed, especially since 1930. Improved marketing facilities through cooperatives and state-organized and state-supported markets, enforcement of quarantine laws, and fertilizer inspection are important accomplishments that have resulted largely from the work of the State Department of Agriculture.

Regardless of the continuing prominence of agriculture in Georgia, manufacturing has increased in importance during the century. The prosperity of the first two decades after 1900 led to increased industrial development. The end of World War I and the 1929 depression slowed this growth, but from the late 1930's, through World War II, to the present day, industrial growth has been steady. Throughout the century, cotton textiles, cottonseed products, fertilizers, processed foods, and lumber and lumber products have been the most important manufactures in Georgia. Atlanta, Savannah, Augusta, Columbus, and Macon are leaders in industry. In textiles, much of Georgia's production is devoted to relatively cheap products. In recent years, a wearing apparel industry has grown up. In timber products, the chief end products are lumber, shingles, and other semifinished items, mostly made of pine. The production of kraft paper from pine is an old industry, but newsprint and better grades of paper are now produced, thanks to the research of Dr. Charles Herty in the 1920's and 1930's. In the production of naval stores, mainly from longleaf pine, Georgia has long been a leader. Several changes have come in the food processing industry. Canning for commercial and home use has increased greatly, especially with the establishment of community canneries in the 1930's and later. Freezing is also used for fruits, vegetables, seafood, poultry, and other items. Candy and soft drinks have remained important industries for the state.

The manufacturing prospect sparked by World War II has continued, and today far more Georgians are engaged in manufacturing and services than in agriculture. The Atlanta area has profited most from this industrial growth, but other cities and smaller towns have also profited from more diversified industry. Atlanta has continued as the southeastern regional capital in industry, government, and service industries; and Savannah has grown in importance as a port and industrial center.

As manufacturing increased in the state, a widespread and efficient transportation system became a necessity. In 1900 internal transportation depended mainly upon the 5000 miles of railroads in the state. River transportation had declined in importance and motor transport had not yet begun. Railway construction and consolidation continued, until in 1928 Georgia had ten main trunk lines and 7049 miles of track. Since that time, there have been further consolidations and a decrease in mileage to about 5000 miles. The policy of state regulation of railroads, begun in the Populist period, has been continued, with main emphasis on supervision of rates and safety precautions.

The century opened with state highway maintenance entirely in local hands and with few standards that could be enforced for road construction and maintenance. The coming of the automobile, however, necessitated considerable road improvement. In 1916 the prison commission was given the duty of supervising a state highway system. A separate highway commission was created a few years later. Funds for state highway construction came at first from automobile license taxes and were apportioned to the counties in accordance with the highway mileage in each.

In 1919 the state itself began road construction, and two years later a tax of one cent per gallon on all gasoline sold was imposed and allocated to the highway commission for road construction. With the increase of the tax to four cents and the great increase in the amount of gasoline sold, the fund amounted to the largest single source of state income in the early 1930's, and highway construction came to be big business and big politics in Georgia. Extensive highway paving began with the second quarter of the century and was carried out on a pay-as-you-go basis. More recently there has been considerable federal aid to highway building, especially the interstate system, completed in the late 1970's.

Commercial aviation became important in Georgia in the 1930's with the building of airfields and the establishment of regular passenger routes and regular airmail schedules. Atlanta, as it had been the railroad center, soon became the aviation center of the state and one of the more important commercial air terminals in the world. The importance of river transportation declined in the twentieth century. Port business at Savannah and Brunswick rose and fell, but generally has been of less value in the twentieth century than it was in the nineteenth. The development of state-owned docks at Savannah has reversed this trend since 1950.

Labor has received considerably more emphasis in the twentieth century than ever before. Previously the state showed little interest in the status of workers. The state's concern had been almost entirely with industrial workers, and farm labor and employees of retail establishments had received little or no consideration. The greatest labor trouble of the period was the textile strike of 1934, during which Governor Eugene Talmadge used the National Guard to prevent picketing, an action for which he was severely criticized by organized labor.

The Department of Commerce and Labor was created in 1911 (labor was separated from commerce in 1937) and charged with improving conditions of industrial workers. In 1920 a workmen's compensation law was enacted which provided for compensation for industrial accidents. A child labor law, setting fourteen as a minimum age for employment in industrial establishments, was passed in 1914; but enforcement was poor for a number of years. In 1900 the work week in manufacturing industries generally averaged between fifty-four and sixty hours. Further reductions came with the New Deal and as a result of federal action. In the 1970's the forty hour week is common.

Wages fluctuated with the business cycle, being high during the two wars and low before and between them. Real wages have risen considerably in the last three decades. Georgia's leading industries do not require highly skilled labor, and hence the workforce for the most part has remained unorganized, with salaries below the national average. In the early 1970's only about 16 percent of the workers were unionized.

Education is another area in which the state has ranked below the national level. Throughout the first quarter of the century, Georgia was near the bottom in the length of school term, the amount of money spent per pupil, the percentage of school-age children enrolled, and other features that indicate a good school system. In all school matters the standards of the Negro schools were much lower than those for whites, and those for whites were considerably below the national average. In 1900 Georgia ranked near the bottom with an illiteracy rate of 52 percent. By 1970 this had been reduced to about 2 percent as a result of conscientious efforts by schools and other agencies. The state passed its first compulsory school attendance law in 1916, but the law had many loopholes, and enforcement remained poor for a long time. In 1900 there were districts where the school term was only forty days a year. By 1915 the average school year was 140 days. A seven-month mandatory school term was prescribed by law in 1935, and a nine-month term in 1952.

Support for public education in Georgia at the opening of the century came almost entirely from the state school fund, which made up about half of the state's expenditure. A few cities had independent school systems financed partially by local taxation, but few counties levied school taxes. In the first quarter of the century the amount of local support increased, until in 1925 only about one-third of the school money came from the state. The next year an equalization fund was created by the legislature to help poorer counties, and this did a great deal toward improving rural education. By the 1940's the trend was again toward more state and less local support. This trend has continued—in the 1970s education accounts for almost half of the state's expenditure.

Attempts to get better education through the consolidation of small schools and the providing of transportation for students began in 1898. Little progress was made, however, until a 1919 law provided financial support to consolidated schools and offered additional funds if a four-year accredited high school was created. The greatest number of consolidations took place in the 1920's and 1930's, virtually eliminating one-teacher white schools. By 1950 many rural counties had only two or three white elementary schools and only one white high school. In 1940 most black schools were still one-teacher, but by 1960 almost no one-teacher schools remained.

At the beginning of the century, the Georgia constitution provided that only elementary and college education could be supported by state funds. High schools, of which there were few, had to be privately or locally supported. A 1907 constitutional amendment allowed state support for high schools, and in 1911 they became an integral part of the public educational system. In the 1920's the State Department of Education secured money to encourage the founding of high schools, and by 1932 every county had a public high school for whites.

In 1913 the state undertook a program designed to secure uniform, approved, and cheap textbooks for all schools. In

1936 the first free textbooks were supplied by the state in primary schools. From this beginning has come the furnishing by the state of all textbooks for public schools.

The passage in 1949 and financing in 1951 of the Minimum Foundation Program of Education brought about a marked improvement in public education. The program was instrumental in constructing adequate buildings, increasing school consolidation, securing adequately trained and paid teachers, and providing Georgia's children with an education that would prepare them for the demands and opportunities of the twentieth century. By 1954, all of the state's secondary schools had twelve grades, and as salaries improved, the difference between white and black teachers' salaries virtually disappeared and the expenditure per pupil became more equitable.

When the U.S. Supreme Court decision in Brown v. Board of Education in 1954 outlawed segregation in public education, another major change in Georgia's educational system began. First, the legislature enacted laws to prevent integration and provided for the abolition of public education if integration were ordered. Many citizens objected to the abolition of public education, and in 1960 the legislature created a special committee headed by John A. Sibley, an Atlanta banker, to study the matter. After holding hearings throughout the state, the committee recommended that Georgia repeal its massive resistance laws and substitute a local option plan.

Then in early January, 1961, the federal district court ordered that two black students be admitted to the University of Georgia. The legislature gave in, and the University remained open. That fall Atlanta began the integration of its public schools, a movement that spread over the state in the next several years. With integration came an increased number of private schools, aimed at maintaining a segregated learning experience.

Also there was increased concern that the schools were not providing students with the basic skills needed for life. A major push to improve reading skills has been made, but the problem is far from solved. Georgia's public schools have changed and improved greatly in the century, but they still have an impossible task—to be all things to all people.

In higher education the century opened with great promise. Walter B. Hill, who became chancellor of the University of Georgia in 1899, gave it badly needed new life. He secured the first annual legislative appropriation for the University and envisioned an institution that would be a valuable service in all phases of state life. He began a program of expansion, which included the founding of professional schools at the University. Unfortunately, Hill died in 1905, before his vision of a great institution was realized. Several additional professional schools were founded during the next decade, and others have followed since. The policy, begun in the late nineteenth century, of founding new branches of the University, which were actually independent schools, continued until there were twenty-six state colleges and twelve district agricultural and mechanical schools in the state. Despite inadequate funds to provide for such a large number of colleges, there was much overlapping of curricula. This confusion ended in 1931, when a single Board of Regents was given control of all state-supported colleges. The Regents immediately reorganized the University System by abolishing a number of small and weak schools, reducing others to junior colleges, and eliminating much duplication of professional education. Private and church-related colleges have declined in number but have increased in enrollment and course offerings. The leaders in graduate and professional education have been the University of Georgia, Georgia Institute of Technology, Emory University (which moved from Oxford to Atlanta in the 1920's), Georgia State University (since 1969), and the Medical College of Georgia. Research, graduate study, and professional work have greatly increased in the last several decades. Growth in college enrollments and physical plants has been very great since 1945.

Having survived the Talmadge purge attempts of 1941 and the curtailments of the war years (1941–1945), public and private colleges experienced rapid growth after 1945. In the early 1950's enrollment in the University System of Georgia was 15,458, but by 1975 it had increased to 110,000. Faculties, research possibilities, and campuses likewise grew remarkably. Despite integration of colleges, both public and private colleges for blacks (especially the Atlanta University Center group) grew in size and usefulness. Despite all this growth and increased funding, Georgia schools at all levels still found themselves below the national average in funding, faculty training, and test scores of students.

Although education has become the most important and expensive service of the state, the older social services inherited from the nineteenth century have continued, and several new ones have been added. For the care of the physically and mentally handicapped, a state mental hospital, a school for the blind, and a school for the deaf have continued. Central State Hospital at Milledgeville is now supplemented by a system of regional mental health centers where outpatient treatment is available. A school for mentally defective children was established at Gracewood in 1919. The asylum and the school at Gracewood have often been caretakers rather than being able to carry on effective treatment. By 1905 all Confederate veterans and their widows could receive state pensions, and there was a Confederate Veterans' Home in Atlanta. About mid-century all veterans were dead, and there are only a few widows still receiving state pensions.

Georgia's prison population increased in the twentieth century. The century opened with mounting criticism of the convict lease system. The main objections voiced were that the lessors made a profit from the prisoners, that there was no attempt at reform, and that many prisoners were cruelly treated and inadequately fed and housed. In 1909 convict leasing was abolished, and prisoners were henceforth retained by the state or in the county work camps, where they were set to work building or repairing roads. Soon many of the same arguments that had been used against the lease system were used against county chain gangs. Adequate supervision or control was often impossible in county camps. Cruel treatment was charged against many wardens. The penitentiary maintained at Milledgeville housed only a small proportion of the state's prisoners. After 1905 a reformatory was maintained to separate delinquent boys from older and more hardened criminals. During Governor Arnall's administration, a new board of corrections was created to have supervision over all state prisoners. Most of the prisoners were soon moved to the new penitentiary at Reidsville, where improved physical facilities made scientific criminology easier to practice than it had been in the old and outdated penitentiary. Despite improved facilities, new methods, and a prison system (which still includes some county work camps), the prison problem is far from solved. Increased numbers of prisoners and rehabilitation are the biggest problems of the 1970's.

(By 1900 many Georgians were sure that statewide prohibition was the only solution to the evils of alcohol. An organized prohibition movement had been gaining strength for a quarter of a century before the first attempt at statewide prohibition failed in 1899. In 1907 a prohibition law was enacted, but enforcement by local officials was largely a failure. The law was tightened and enforcement improved until by 1919, when prohibition became national, it was illegal to manufacture, sell, or possess intoxicating liquor in Georgia.

The enactment of prohibition legislation did not end the manufacture or consumption of intoxicating liquors. After the repeal of national prohibition in 1933, many favored repeal of Georgia's law. In 1935 repeal was defeated, but beer and wine were legalized. In 1938 local option was enacted, and urban counties began to go wet. In the years since, the general tendency has been for more areas to become wet, a move greatly aided by a recent law allowing towns and cities to become wet regardless of what the county does. In many respects the drug problem of the 1960's and 1970's has paralleled the liquor problem of earlier days.

Although the government has long been concerned with health and the control of communicable diseases, Georgia had no governmental agency responsible for the general oversight of the physical well-being of its citizens until a state board of health was established in 1903. County boards were prescribed by law in 1914. These state and county boards were directed to supervise public sanitation, preventive medicine, and the control of communicable diseases, especially when the latter threaten to attain epidemic proportions. The state board acts as a central clearing agency and formulates policy for statewide application. State and local inspectors have done much to improve sanitary conditions in food-handling establishments, to maintain standards for water and food supplies, and to enforce environmental controls for the protection of the public health. The most complete public health services are carried out in the cities, while many rural communities still have inadequate services. The State Health Department encourages preventive medicine by sending mobile clinics throughout the state, especially to schools. The fights against hookworm and pellagra early in the century are good examples of educational campaigns that resulted in improved health conditions. Perhaps the greatest work has been done in the detection of tuberculosis. Overall there has been a decrease in epidemic diseases in the twentieth century. Public health measures have helped to reduce infant mortality, to increase the life span, and to make for healthier Georgians. Georgia has fewer doctors per capita than the national average, and those who do practice in the state tend to concentrate in the cities, leaving many rural areas without adequate medical care.

Welfare activities were mainly private or conducted by local governments until the 1930's, when federal-state cooperative programs began. The major social welfare programs today include aid to dependent children, the aged, the disabled, and the blind, and the Medicare and Medicaid programs. In the 1970's about one Georgian in ten gets some type of welfare aid.

School integration in the 1960's marked the beginning of securing racial equality. Dr. Martin Luther King, Jr., aided by the 1964 Civil Rights Act and the 1965 Voting Rights Act, was instrumental in bringing about many of the changes of that decade. Congressman Andrew Young in 1972 and Mayor Maynard Jackson in 1973, both from Atlanta, were widely publicized blacks in high office, but often it was the positions that blacks increasingly occupied in local governments, school boards, and businesses that were more important. The 1960s also saw the desegregation of public transportation, hotels, restaurants, and other services.

World War II brought increased mobility to the American people, and corporate growth since the war has continued the trend. Georgia's population increased from 3,123,000 in 1940 to 5,000,000 in 1978. In the same years rural population declined from about 65 percent to about 35 percent, with only 10 percent of the rural population engaged in agriculture in 1974. In the same years, black population decreased from about 33⅓ percent to about 25 percent of the total population.

By the 1960's life styles had changed to the point that there was little difference between urban and rural living so far as creature comforts were concerned. Most Georgians had electricity, radio, television, telephones, indoor plumbing, air conditioning, paved roads, and automobiles. WSB, in Atlanta, was Georgia's first radio station in 1922 and first television station in 1948 and has been a leader in both fields of mass communication, which has done much to change the life style in the state. Atlanta has also become a center for spectator sports, with the Falcons (football), the Braves (baseball), the Hawks (basketball) and the Flames (hockey)/Orchestra, opera, ballet, and theater are increasingly available over the state.

The architecture of Georgia's new buildings reflects the standardization of the mid-twentieth century, whether it be suburban housing for the middle class, fast food establishments, or governmental buildings. But the average Georgian has been better housed in recent years than ever before. Peachtree Center in Atlanta is among the best of the new urban architecture, but Georgia's real architectural marvel is Savannah, where the community has restored many nineteenth-century houses and changed deteriorating areas into first-class residential districts again.

Religion has retained the basic pattern of the nineteenth century: church membership is high, and the majority of the state's churches are protestant. Many rural churches have declined or been abandoned as members moved away, but the members took their fundamentalist views into the cities with them.)

One field in which modern-day standardization is not obvious is literature. Frank L. Stanton is probably Georgia's best-loved twentieth-century poet. Other poets of merit are Byron Herbert Reece, Daniel Whitehead Hickey, and Ernest Hartsock. In prose, Margaret Mitchell's *Gone with the Wind*—the recipient of a Pulitzer Prize in 1936—is by far the best-known work produced in or about Georgia in the century. Close to her is Joel Chandler Harris, whose Uncle Remus stories say so much about human nature. Three women who wrote in and about Georgia were Corra Harris, *A Circuit Rider's Wife*; Caroline Miller, *Lamb in His Bosom* (Pulitzer Prize, 1934); and Lillian Smith, *Strange Fruit*. Harry Stillwell Edwards had a nostalgic look at a bygone day with *Eneas Africanus,* while Erskine Caldwell in *Tobacco Road* showed much of the seamy side of life. Flannery O'Connor's grotesque fiction is well known. Berry Fleming writes both history and historical fiction. E. Merton Coulter and Bell Irvin Wiley are among the state's best-known historians.

In this century it is safe to summarize with the statement that Georgia's material environment has changed more than her people. The basic conflict for many, a desire to cling to the old and yet reap the benefit of the new, often makes progress slow. There is an innate conservatism often balanced by liberal change. There is both change and progress; people differ about the amount and the direction, and which is which, but most agree that at least a part of the change is progress.

Bibliography

The books listed below are the most well known and most easily accessible works of Georgia history and will be of use to readers who wish to pursue some subject in more detail than it is treated here. A more complete bibliography is contained in Kenneth Coleman et al., *A History of Georgia* (Athens, 1977), and Arthur Ray Rowland and James E. Dorsey, *A Bibliography of the Writings of Georgia History, 1900–1970* (Spartanburg, S.C., 1978).

GENERAL WORKS ON GEORGIA HISTORY

Bonner, James C. *A History of Georgia Agriculture, 1732–1759,* Athens, 1964.

Coleman, Kenneth, et al. *A History of Georgia,* Athens, 1977.

Collections of the Georgia Historical Society. 19 vols. Savannah, 1840–1976.

Cooper, Walter G. *The Story of Georgia.* 4 vols. New York, 1938.

Coulter, E. Merton. *Georgia: A Short History.* Chapel Hill, 1947, 1960.

Griffith, Louis T., and John E. Talmadge. *Georgia Journalism, 1763–1950.* Athens, 1951.

Georgia Historical Quarterly. Published by the Georgia Historical Society. Savannah, since 1917.

Heath, Milton S. *Constructive Liberalism: The Role of the State in Economic Development in Georgia to 1860.* Cambridge, Mass., 1954.

Howell, Clark. *History of Georgia.* 4 vols. Chicago, 1926.

Johnson, Amanda. *Georgia as Colony and State.* Atlanta, 1938.

Knight, Lucian Lamar. *A Standard History of Georgia and Georgians.* 6 vols. Chicago, 1917.

Martin, Harold H. *Georgia: A History.* New York, 1977.

Orr, Dorothy. *A History of Education in Georgia.* Chapel Hill, 1950.

Range, Willard. *A Century of Georgia Agriculture, 1850–1950.* Athens, 1954.

Saye, Albert B. *New Viewpoints in Georgia History.* Athens, 1943.

———. *A Constitutional History of Georgia, 1732–1945.* Athens, 1948, 1970.

CHAPTER I. COLONIAL GEORGIA

Abbot, W. W. *The Royal Governors of Georgia, 1754–1775.* Chapel Hill, 1959.

Bolton, Herbert E., and Mary Ross. *The Debatable Land.* Berkeley, Calif., 1925.

Candler, Allen D., et al, eds. *The Colonial Records of the State of Georgia.* 28 vols. to date. Atlanta and Athens, 1904–78.

Coleman, Kenneth. *Colonial Georgia.* New York, 1976.

Corry, John P. *Indian Affairs in Georgia, 1732–1756.* Philadelphia, 1936.

Davis, Harold C. *The Fledgling Province.* Chapel Hill, 1976.

Ettinger, Amos A. *James Edward Oglethorpe, Imperial Idealist.* Oxford, 1936.

Flippin, Percy S. "Royal Government in Georgia, 1752–1776," *Georgia Historical Quarterly* 8–13: (1924–29).

Jones, Charles C., Jr. *The History of Georgia.* 2 vols. Boston, 1883.

Lanning, John T. *The Diplomatic History of Georgia: A Study of the Epoch of Jenkins' Ear.* Chapel Hill, 1936.

———. *The Spanish Missions of Georgia.* Chapel Hill, 1935.

Lovell, Caroline C. *The Golden Isles of Georgia.* Boston, 1932.

McCain, James R. *Georgia as a Proprietary Province.* Boston, 1917.

Spalding, Phinizy. *Oglethorpe in America.* Chicago, 1977.

Stevens, William B. *A History of Georgia.* 2 vols. New York, 1847–59.

Strickland, Reba C. *Religion and the State in Georgia in the Eighteenth Century.* New York, 1939.

Temple, Sarah B. G., and Kenneth Coleman. *Georgia Journeys.* Athens, 1961.

CHAPTER II. GEORGIA IN THE
REVOLUTION

Jones, Stevens, and Strickland from Chapter I.

Coleman, Kenneth. *The American Revolution in Georgia, 1763–1798.* Athens, 1958.

Candler, Allen D., ed. *The Revolutionary Records of the State of Georgia.* 3 vols. Atlanta, 1908.

Jenkins, Charles F. *Button Gwinnett, Signer of the Declaration of Independence.* New York, 1926.

Johnston, Elizabeth L. *Recollections of a Georgia Loyalist.* New York, 1901.

Jones, Charles C., Jr. *Biographical Sketches of the Delegates from Georgia to the Continental Congress.* Boston, 1891.

Lawrence, Alexander A. *Storm Over Savannah: The Story of Count d'Estaing and the Siege of the Town in 1779.* Athens, 1951.

CHAPTER III. ANTE-BELLUM GEORGIA,
1785–1860

Coulter, E. Merton. *College Life in the Old South.* New York, 1928; rpt., Athens, 1951.
———. *Georgia's Disputed Ruins.* Chapel Hill, 1937.
———. *Thomas Spalding of Sapelo.* University, La., 1940.
Flanders, Bertram H. *Early Georgia Magazines, Literary Periodicals to 1865.* Athens, 1944.
Flanders, Ralph B. *Plantation Slavery in Georgia.* Chapel Hill, 1933.
Foreman, Grant. *Indian Removal: The Emigration of the Five Civilized Tribes of Indians.* Norman, Oklahoma, 1932.
Kemble, Frances Anne. *Journal of a Residence on a Georgian Plantation in 1838–1839.* New York, 1863, 1961.
McLendon, Samuel G. *History of the Public Domain of Georgia.* Atlanta, 1924.
Malone, Henry T. *Cherokees of the Old South.* Athens, 1956.
Montgomery, Horace. *Cracker Parties.* Baton Rouge, 1950.
Murray, Paul. *The Whig Party in Georgia.* Chapel Hill, 1948.
Phillips, Ulrich B. *Georgia and State Rights.* Washington, 1902.
———. *A History of Transportation in the Eastern Cotton Belt to 1860.* New York, 1908.
———. *The Life of Robert Toombs.* New York, 1913.
Shryock, R. H. *Georgia and the Union in 1850.* Durham, N.C., 1926.
Starkey, Marion L. *The Cherokee Nation.* New York, 1946.
Von Abele, Rudolph. *Alexander H. Stephens.* New York, 1946.
Wade, John D. *Augustus Baldwin Longstreet.* New York, 1924; rpt., Athens, 1969.

CHAPTER IV. SLAVERY, SECESSION,
AND THE CIVIL WAR

Phillips and Shryock from Chapter III.
Andrews, Eliza Frances. *The War-Time Journal of a Georgia Girl, 1864–1865.* New York, 1908; rpt., Macon, 1960.
Avery, Issac W. *The History of the State of Georgia, 1850–1881.* New York, 1881.
Brantley, Rabun L. *Georgia Journalism of the Civil War Period.* Nashville, 1929.
Bryan, T. Conn. *Confederate Georgia.* Athens, 1953.
Candler, Allen D., ed. *The Confederate Records of the State of Georgia.* 5 vols. Atlanta, 1909–11.
Flippin, Percy S. *Herschel V. Johnson of Georgia.* Richmond, 1931.

Hill, Louise B. *Joseph E. Brown and the Confederacy.* Chapel Hill, 1939.
LeConte, Joseph. *'Ware Sherman: A Journal of Three Months' Personal Experience in the Last Days of the Confederacy.* Berkeley, Calif., 1937.
Lunt, Dolly S. *A Woman's Wartime Journal.* Macon, 1927.
Parks, Joseph H. *Joseph E. Brown of Georgia.* Baton Rouge, 1977.
Pearce, Haywood, J., Jr. *Benjamin H. Hill.* Chicago, 1928.
Richardson, E. Ramsay. *Little Aleck, A Life of Alexander H. Stephens.* Indianapolis, 1932.

CHAPTER V. RECONSTRUCTION, BOURBONISM, AND POPULISM, 1865-1900

Avery, Hill, Parks, Pearce, and Richardson from Chapter IV.
Arnett, Alex M. *The Populist Movement in Georgia.* New York, 1922.
Brooks, Robert P. *The Agrarian Revolution in Georgia, 1865-1912.* Madison, Wis., 1914.
Conway, Alan. *The Reconstruction of Georgia.* Minneapolis, 1966.
Felton, Mrs. William H. *My Memoirs of Georgia Politics.* Atlanta, 1911.
Harris, Julia C. *Joel Chandler Harris, Editor and Essayist.* Chapel Hill, 1931.
Harris, N. E. *Autobiography.* Macon, 1925.
Leigh, Frances B. *Ten Years on a Georgia Plantation since the War.* London, 1883.
Nixon, Raymond B. *Henry W. Grady: Spokesman of the New South.* New York, 1943.
Range, Willard. *A Century of Georgia Agriculture, 1850-1950.* Athens, 1954.
Thompson, C. Mildred. *Reconstruction in Georgia: Economic, Social, Political, 1865-1872.* New York, 1915.
Woodward, C. Vann. *Tom Watson: Agrarian Rebel.* New York, 1938.

CHAPTER VI. TWENTIETH-CENTURY GEORGIA

Brooks, Felton, J. C. Harris, N. E. Harris, Range, and Woodward from Chapter V.
Akioka, Lorena M., and Carolyn S. Hudgins, eds. *1976 Georgia Statistical Abstract.* Athens, 1976.
Anderson, William. *The Wild Man from Sugar Creek: The Political Career of Eugene Talmadge.* Baton Rouge, 1975.
Bartley, Numan V. *From Thurmond to Wallace: Political Tendencies in Georgia, 1948-1968.* Baltimore, 1970.
Blecher, John C., and Imogene Dean, eds. *Georgia Today: Facts and Trends.* Athens, 1960.

Byers, Tracy. *Martha Berry, the Sunday Lady of Possum Trot.* New York, 1932.

Georgia: A Guide to its Towns and Countryside. Athens, 1940.

Gosnell, Cullen B., and C. David Anderson. *The Government and Administration of Georgia.* New York, 1956.

Grantham, Dewey W., Jr. *Hoke Smith and the Politics of the New South.* Baton Rouge, 1958.

Hughes, M. Clyde. *County Government in Georgia.* Athens, 1944.

Meadows, J. C. *Modern Georgia.* Athens, 1954.

Pound, Merritt B., and Melvin E. Thompson. *Georgia Citizenship.* Richmond, 1940.

Raper, Arthur F. *Tenants of the Almighty.* New York, 1943.

Steed, Hal. *Georgia, Unfinished State.* New York, 1942.

Index

Abolitionists, 48
Academies, 42
Adams, John Quincy, 34
Agriculture, colonial, 13-14; *1790-1860*, 38-40; Civil War, 59-60; Reconstruction, 75-76; *1872-1900*, 86-87; twentieth century, 106-7; education, 107; State Dept. of, 87
Alliance, Farmers', 82-84
Amusements, 45-46
Andersonville Prison, 66
Andrews, James J., raid, 57
Ann, frigate, 5
Arnall, Ellis Gibbs, 99-103
Arp, Bill, 63, 79
Ashe, John, 23
Assembly, Trustees, 10; royal, 11
Atlanta, 58, 66-67, 72, 77, 81-82, 87-88
Atlanta Constitution, 81, 88, 94
Atlanta-Savannah campaign, 67-68
Augusta, 6, 9, 22-25, 33, 58
Aviation, 109

Banking, 41, 77
Bell, John, 50
Berrien, John M., 37, 49
Bethesda Orphanage, 14
Blind, school for, 44, 93, 114
Bloody Marsh, battle of, 7
Bolzius, John Martin, 6
Bourbonism, 80-82, 87-89
Bray, Thomas, 2-3
Breckinridge, John C., 50-51
Briar Creek, battle of, 23
Brown, Joseph E., 50-56, 58, 60, 62, 66-71, 74, 81, 82, 88
Brown, Thomas, 24
Brownson, Nathan, 25
Bull, William, 5
Bulloch, Archibald, 19, 20
Bullock, Rufus B., 72-74, 80

Caldwell, Erskine, 118
Campbell, Archibald, 22-23
Canals, 38
Carmichael, James V., 101
Carolina, 2, 5, 13
Carter, Jimmy, 103-4
Charity colonists, 5, 6, 10, 11
Chattanooga-Atlanta campaign, 65-67
Cherokee Indians, 34-36
Cherokee Nation v. Georgia, 35
Cherokee Phoenix, 35
Chivers, Thomas Holly, 46
Christian Index, 46
A Circuit Rider's Wife, 118
Clark, John, 36
Clark Party, 36
Clarke, Elijah, 23, 24
Clayton, Augustin S., 36
Cobb, Howell, 49, 52, 55
Cobb, Thomas R. R., 44, 51, 52
Colonists, selection of, 5
Colquitt, Alfred H., 81, 82, 86
Columbus, 33, 58
Committee of correspondence, 16-17
Compromise of *1850*, 49
Conscription, Civil War, 61-62
Confederate veterans, 92-93, 114
Constitution of Georgia, *1776*, 20; *1777*, 21; *1789*, 27, 29; *1798*, 29; *1865*, 69; *1868*, 71-72, 80; *1877*, 80-81, 83, 104; *1945*, 100-101
Constitution of U.S., adopted, 27, 29
Constitutional Union Party, 49-51
Continental Congress, 17, 18, 19, 26
Convict lease system, 90
Cotton States and International Exposition, 81, 88
Coulter, E. Merton, 118
Council of Safety, 18-19
County creation and consolidation, 21, 29, 30, 33, 104-5

Courts, 21, 104; juvenile, 104
Crawford, William H., 36
Creek Indians, 3, 6, 27, 32–34

Darien, 6, 57
Davis, Jefferson, 52–55, 62, 66
Deaf, school for, 44, 93, 114
DeBrahm, John Gerar William, 13
Debtors, 2–3, 5, 11
Declaration of Independence, 20
Democratic Party, 37, 49–50, 80,
    83–85, 93; Independents, 82
Deserters, Civil War, 61–62
De Soto, Hernando, 1
d'Estaing, Count Henri, 23
Dooly, John, 23

Ebenezer, 6, 10
Economic affairs, colonial, 9, 14;
    Revolution, 27; *1790–1860*, 37–
    41; Civil War, 55, 56, 57–61; Re-
    construction, 74–78; *1872–1900*,
    85–89; twentieth century, 106–10
Education, *1790–1860*, 42–44; Civil
    War, 63–64; Reconstruction, 72,
    78–79; *1872–1900*, 90–92; twen-
    tieth century, 99–100, 110–14;
    higher, 42–43, 71, 78, 91–92,
    99–100, 112–113
Edwards, Harry Stillwell, 118
Egmont, Earl of, 3
Elliott, Stephen, 64
Ellis, Henry, 12
Eneas Africanus, 118

Farmer relief, 82–85
Felton, William H., 82
Few, Benjamin, 24
Few, William, 24
Fifteenth Amendment, 73
Fleming, Berry, 118
Fletcher v. Peck, 32
Florida, 1–2, 7–8, 22–23, 25, 32
Forrest, Nathan Bedford, 57
Forsyth, John, 36–37
Fort Pulaski, 57
Fourteenth Amendment, 72, 73
Frank, Leo, 95
Frederica, 7, 10
Freedmen's Bureau, 75
French at Savannah, 23

Garrison, William Lloyd, 48
George, Walter F., 98, 102
Georgia Historical Society, 46
Georgia, physical geography, 1
Georgia Platform, 49
Georgia Scenes, 46
Georgia, state finances, 55–56, 73–
    74, 77, 98–99
Germans, 4–5, 13
Gold discovery, 35, 77
Gone with the Wind, 117
Gordon, John B., 72, 81, 82, 84
Goulding, Francis R., 46
Grady, Henry W., 81, 82, 88
Graham, John, 13
Grandfather clause, 95
Grange, 82–83
Greene, Nathanael, 25
Griffin, Marvin, 102
Guerrilla warfare in Revolution, 24
Guale, 1–2
Gunn, James, 31
Gwinnett, Button, 20–21

Habersham, James, 17
Habersham, James, Jr., 17
Habersham, John, 17
Hall, Lyman, 17–19
Harris, Corra, 118
Harris, Joel Chandler, 63, 117
Hart, Nancy, 24
Hayne, Paul Hamilton, 79
Health, public, 115–16
Herty, Charles, 108
Hickey, Daniel Whitehead, 117
Highways, 37, 109
Hill, Benjamin H., 50–51, 55, 74, 81
Hill, Joshua, 72, 74
Hood, John B., 66
Houstoun, John, 19, 22
Howe, Robert, 22
Howell, Clark, 94
Howell, Evan P., 88

Illiteracy, 42
Indian land cessions, 29–30, 32,
    33–36
Indians, relations with, 2–3, 5–7, 13,
    29–30, 32–36
International Cotton Exposition, 81

INDEX

Jackson, Andrew, 32, 35, 37
Jackson, James, 31, 36
Jefferson, Thomas, 36
Jenkins, Charles J., 69–70, 72
Jews, 4, 6, 95–96
Johnson, Andrew, 69
Johnson, Herschel V., 51, 55, 70
Johnson, James, 69
Johnson, Leroy, 103
Johnston, Joseph E., 66
Johnston, Richard Malcolm, 79
Jones, Charles C., Jr., 79
Jones, Noble, 17
Jones, Noble W., 16, 17, 19
Journalism, 46–47, 62–63, 79
Juvenile courts, 104

Kansas-Nebraska Bill, 50
Kettle Creek, battle of, 23
King, Martin L., Jr., 116
Knights of Labor, 89
Know-Nothing Party, 50
Ku Klux Klan, 73, 95–96

Labor conditions, 89, 97–98, 109–10
Lamb in His Bosom, 118
Land cessions, 13, 29–30, 32–36
Land granting, 8, 10, 14, 25–26, 30–33
Land speculation, 30–32
Langworthy, Edward, 45
Legislative reapportionment, 103
Libraries, 45
Lincoln, Abraham, 51
Lincoln, Benjamin, 22–23
Literature, 45–47, 79, 117–18
Livingston, L. F., 84
Longstreet, Augustus Baldwin, 46
Louisville, 33
Loyalists, *see* Tories
Lumpkin, Joseph Henry, 43

Macon, 33, 58
Maddox, Lester, 103
Manufacturing, *1790–1860*, 40–41; Civil War, 57–59; *1872–1900*, 88–89; twentieth century, 107–8
McCall, Hugh, 46
McIntosh, Lachlan, 21
Meade, George G., 72
Medicine, 43
Mental Illness, care for, 44, 93, 114

Mercantilism, 2–4, 8–9, 11, 15
Mexican War, 48–49
Midway, 13
Milledgeville, 33, 67
Miller, Caroline, 118
Miller, H. V. M., 72, 74
Missouri Compromise, 48
Mitchell, Margaret, 117
Moravians, 6
Morrill Land Grant Act, 78, 91
Mulberry trees, 10
Munitions manufacture, 52, 58

Nashville Convention, 49
Negro, churches, 79; education, 40, 78–79, 84, 91–92, 110–14; free, 40; in politics, 82–85, 94–95, 101–3, 116; Reconstruction, 70–80; *1960's–1970's*, 116; *see* Slavery.
New Deal, 97–98, 106, 110
New Echota, 35
New York, Treaty of, *1790*, 29–30
Newspapers, Revolutionary, 19; *1790–1860*, 46–47; Civil War, 62–63; Reconstruction, 79
Nisbet, Eugenius A., 50
North Georgia Agricultural College, 78
Northen, William J., 84
Nullification, 36–37

O'Connor, Flannery, 118
Oglethorpe, James Edward, 2–10; regiment, 7–8
Orr, Gustavus J., 91

Parishes, 12
Percival, John Viscount, 3
Pickens, Andrew, 23
Pierce, George Foster, 64
Plantations, *see* Agriculture
Political parties, state, 36–37
Poor-school fund, 42
Pope, John, 71, 72
Population, 10, 13, 30, 33, 116–17
Populist Party, 84–85, 94
Prevost, Augustine, 22–23
Primary elections, 84, 95, 104
Prisons, 44–45, 52, 67, 90, 100, 114–15

Proclamation of *1763*, 15
Prohibition, 8–9, 84, 90, 115
Provincial congress, 17–19, 20
Public education, *see* Education
Pulitzer Prize, 117, 118
Puritans, St. John's Parish, 13, 17–20

Queensborough, 13

Rabenhorst, Christian, 6
Railroad commission, 94
Railroads, *see* Transportation
Reconstruction, Congressional, 70–74
Reece, Byron Herbert, 117
Religion, colonial, 10–11; *1790–1860*, 44; Civil War, 64–65; Reconstruction, 79; *1872–1900*, 92; twentieth century, 117
Republicans, 71–74, 80, 93
Revolutionary War, causes, 15–20; results, 25–28
Reynolds, John, 12
River transportation, 37–38
Rivers, Eurith D., 98–99
Rules and Regulations of *1776*, 20
Russell, Richard B., Jr., 96, 98

St. Augustine, 1–2, 21–22
St. Catherines Island, 1
St. George's Parish, 18
St. John's Parish, 13
St. Simons Island, 7
Salzburgers, 5–6, 9, 10
Sanders, Carl, 102
Savannah, 5, in Revolution, 17, 22–25, 29; in Civil War, 56–58, 67–68
Scotch Highlanders, 6, 9, 19
Scotch-Irish, 13, 19
Secession, 50–53
Segregation, 103, 112
Sequoyah, 34
Share-croppers, 86
Sherman, William T., 65–68
Silk production, 3, 8–9
Slaton, John M., 95
Slavery, 8, 9–10, 14, 38–39, 40, 44; *1790–1860*, 48–50; Civil War, 60–61; abolished, 69; *see* Negro
Smith, Charles H., 63, 79
Smith, Hoke, 94–95

Smith, James M., 80, 91
Smith, Lillian, 118
Social services, 92–93, 114, 116
Soldiers, Confederate, 52–56, 61–62, 64–65; Continental, 22
South Carolina, 15, 20, 27, 51
Southern Cultivator, 46, 63
Southern Field and Fireside, 63
Southern Rights Party, 49–50
Spain, 2–3, 7–8, 30
Spanish missions, 1
Speer, Emory, 82
Stamp Act, 15–16
Stanton, Frank L., 117
State Rights Party, 36–37
Stephens, Alexander H., 49, 52, 67, 70, 74, 81, 82
Stephens, Linton, 55
Stephens, William, 10
Stevens, William B., 46
Strange Fruit, 118
Streight, Abel D., raid, 57
Sugar Act, 15

Talmadge, Eugene, 96–101
Talmadge, Herman E., 101–3
Tariff, 36–37
Tattnall, Josiah, 56
Taxation, 15–16, 55–56, 105
Terry, Alfred H., 73
Texas, 48–49
Theater, 45
Thirteenth amendment, 69
Thompson, Melvin E., 102
Thompson, William Tappan, 46
Tillson, David, 75
Tobacco Road, 118
Tomo-Chi-Chi, 5, 6
Tondee's Tavern meetings, 17
Toombs, Robert, 49–52, 55, 81
Tories, 21, 25
Townshend Revenue Acts, 16
Trade, 14–15, 41
Transportation, *1790–1860*, 37–38; Civil War, 57, 59; Reconstruction, 76–77; twentieth century, 108–9
Troup, George M., 34–36
Troup Party, 36–37
Trustees, 3–5, 8–11
Trustees' Garden, 8
Turner, Joseph Addison, 63

Uncle Remus stories, 117-18
Union Party, 36-37
Union Society, 44
United States, relations with, 17-19, 26, 30, 47

Vandiver, Ernest, 102
Veterans, Civil War, 70, 92-93
Voting qualifications, 12, 21, 29, 70-71, 94, 95, 100-103

Walton, George, 22, 24
War of *1812*, 32
War of Jenkins' Ear, 7-8
War of the Spanish Succession, 2
Watson, Thomas E., 84-85, 94-96
Wayne, Anthony, 25
Webster, Daniel, 49
Wesley, Charles, 11

Wesley, John, 11
Wesleyan College, 43, 63
Wheeler, Joseph, 67
Whig Party, 36-37, 49-50
Whigs, 19-21, 26
Wilde, Richard Henry, 46
Wiley, Bell Irvin, 118
Wilmot Proviso, 49
Wine production, 9
Worcester v. Georgia, 35
World War I, 95
Wright, James, 12, 13, 14, 16-19, 23-24

Yamacraw Bluff, 5
Yazoo Land Fraud, 31-32
Young, Andrew, 116

Zubly, John J., 19

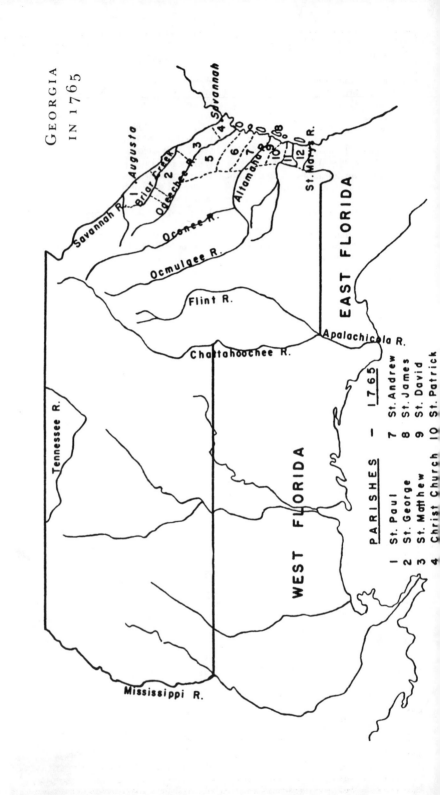

GEORGIA IN 1765

Savannah R.
Augusta
Briar Creek
Ogeechee R.
Savannah
Oconee R.
Ocmulgee R.
Altamaha R.
St. Marys R.
Flint R.
Apalachicola R.
Chattahoochee R.
Tennessee R.
Mississippi R.

EAST FLORIDA

WEST FLORIDA

PARISHES — 1765

1 St. Paul   7 St. Andrew
2 St. George   8 St. James
3 St. Matthew   9 St. David
4 Christ Church 10 St. Patrick

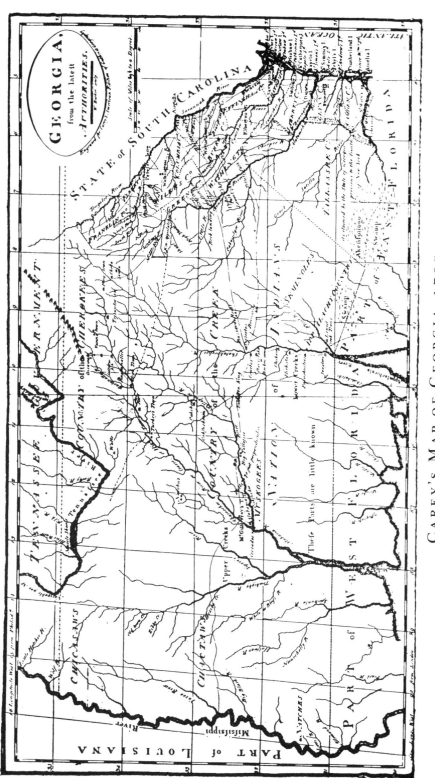

CAREY'S MAP OF GEORGIA, 1795

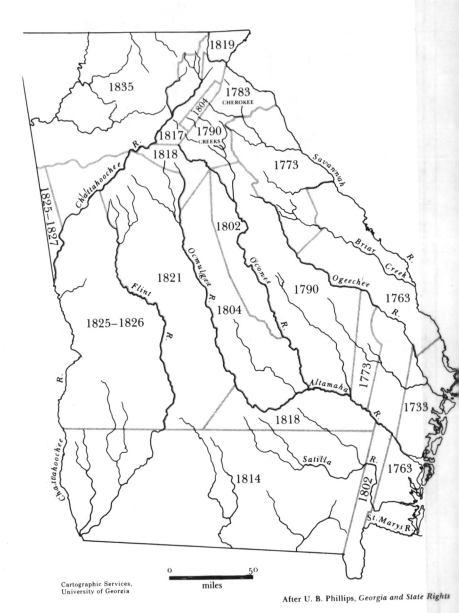

1819

1835

1783
CHEROKEE

1804

1817 1790
CREEKS

1818

1773

Chattahoochee R.

1825–1827

Savannah

1802

Briar Creek R.

1821

Ocmulgee R.

Oconee

Ogeechee

1790

1763
R.

Flint

1804

R.

1825–1826

R.

Altamaha

1773

1733

1818

R.

Satilla

R.

1763

Chattahoochee R.

1814

1802

St. Marys R.

0   50
miles

Cartographic Services,
University of Georgia

After U. B. Phillips, *Georgia and State Rights*

INDIAN CESSIONS IN GEORGIA

LEGEND

★ STATE CAPITAL

◉ COUNTY SEAT

ALL OTHER PLACES HAVING 10,000 OR MORE POPULATION ○

GEORGIA: COUNTIES, PRINCIPAL CITIES, MOUNTAINS, AND RIVERS